# THE CATCHER IN THE RYE

*J. D. Salinger*

SPARK PUBLISHING

122 Fifth Avenue
New York, NY 10011
www.sparknotes.com

ISBN 978-1-4114-6947-1

Please submit changes or report errors to www.sparknotes.com/errors.

Printed in Canada

11

# CONTENTS

# Context

JEROME DAVID SALINGER WAS BORN in New York City in
1919. The son of a wealthy cheese importer, Salinger grew
up in a fashionable neighborhood in Manhattan and spent
his youth being shuttled between various prep schools before his parents finally settled on the Valley Forge Military
Academy in 1934. He graduated from Valley Forge in 1936
and attended a number of colleges, including Columbia University,
but did not graduate from any of them. While at Columbia, Salinger
took a creative writing class in which he excelled, cementing the
interest in writing that he had maintained since his teenage years.
Salinger had his first short story published in 1940; he continued to
write as he joined the army and fought in Europe during World War
II. Upon his return to the United States and civilian life in 1946, Salinger wrote more stories, publishing them in many respected maga-
zines. In 1951, Salinger published his only full-length novel, *The
Catcher in the Rye,* which propelled him onto the national stage.

Many events from Salinger's early life appear in *The Catcher in
the Rye.* For instance, Holden Caulfield moves from prep school to
prep school, is threatened with military school, and knows an older
Columbia student. In the novel, such autobiographical details are
transplanted into a post–World War II setting. *The Catcher in the
Rye* was published at a time when the burgeoning American indus-
trial economy made the nation prosperous and entrenched social
rules served as a code of conformity for the younger generation. Because Salinger used slang and profanity in his text and because he
discussed adolescent sexuality in a complex and open way, many
readers were offended, and *The Catcher in the Rye* provoked great
controversy upon its release. Some critics argued that the book was
not serious literature, citing its casual and informal tone as evidence.
The book was—and continues to be banned in some communities,
and it consequently has been thrown into the center of debates about
First Amendment rights, censorship, and obscenity in literature.

Though controversial, the novel appealed to a great number of
people. It was a hugely popular bestseller and general critical success.
Salinger's writing seemed to tap into the emotions of readers in an
unprecedented way. As countercultural revolt began to grow during
the 1950s and 1960s, *The Catcher in the Rye* was frequently read as

a tale of an individual's alienation within a heartless world. Holden seemed to stand for young people everywhere, who felt themselves beset on all sides by pressures to grow up and live their lives according to the rules, to disengage from meaningful human connection, and to restrict their own personalities and conform to a bland cultural norm. Many readers saw Holden Caulfield as a symbol of pure, unfettered individuality in the face of cultural oppression.

In the same year that *The Catcher in the Rye* appeared, Salinger published a short story in *The New Yorker* magazine called "A Perfect Day for Bananafish," which proved to be the first in a series of stories about the fictional Glass family. Over the next decade, other "Glass" stories appeared in the same magazine: "Franny," "Zooey," and "Raise High the Roof-Beam, Carpenters." These and other stories are available in the only other books Salinger published besides *The Catcher in the Rye*: *Nine Stories* (1953), *Franny and Zooey* (1961), and *Raise High the Roof-Beam, Carpenters and Seymour: An Introduction* (1963). Though *Nine Stories* received some critical acclaim, the critical reception of the later stories was hostile. Critics generally found the Glass siblings to be ridiculously and insufferably precocious and judgmental.

Beginning in the early 1960s, as his critical reputation waned, Salinger began to publish less and to disengage from society. In 1965, after publishing another Glass story ("Hapworth 26, 1924") that was widely reviled by critics, he withdrew almost completely from public life, a stance he has maintained up to the present. This reclusiveness, ironically, has made Salinger even more famous, transforming him into a cult figure. To some degree, Salinger's cult status has overshadowed, or at least tinged, many readers' perceptions of his work. As a recluse, Salinger, for many, embodies much the same spirit as his precocious, wounded characters, and many readers view author and characters as the same being. Such a reading of Salinger's work clearly oversimplifies the process of fiction writing and the relationship between the author and his creations. But, given Salinger's iconoclastic behavior, the general view that Salinger is himself a sort of Holden Caulfield is understandable.

The few brief public statements that Salinger has made suggest that he continues to write stories to this day, implying that the majority of his works may not appear until after his death. Meanwhile, there are signs that readers are becoming more favorably disposed toward Salinger's later writings, meaning that *The Catcher in the Rye* may one day be seen as part of a much larger literary whole.

# Plot Overview

THE CATCHER IN THE RYE is set around the 1950s and is narrated by a young man named Holden Caulfield. Holden is not specific about his location while he's telling the story, but he makes it clear that he is undergoing treatment in a mental hospital or sanatorium. The events he narrates take place in the few days between the end of the fall school term and Christmas, when Holden is sixteen years old.

Holden's story begins on the Saturday following the end of classes at the Pencey prep school in Agerstown, Pennsylvania. Pencey is Holden's fourth school; he has already failed out of three others. At Pencey, he has failed four out of five of his classes and has received notice that he is being expelled, but he is not scheduled to return home to Manhattan until Wednesday. He visits his elderly history teacher, Spencer, to say goodbye, but when Spencer tries to reprimand him for his poor academic performance, Holden becomes annoyed.

Back in the dormitory, Holden is further irritated by his unhygienic neighbor, Ackley, and by his own roommate, Stradlater. Stradlater spends the evening on a date with Jane Gallagher, a girl whom Holden used to date and whom he still admires. During the course of the evening, Holden grows increasingly nervous about Stradlater's taking Jane out, and when Stradlater returns, Holden questions him insistently about whether he tried to have sex with her. Stradlater teases Holden, who flies into a rage and attacks Stradlater. Stradlater pins Holden down and bloodies his nose. Holden decides that he's had enough of Pencey and will go to Manhattan three days early, stay in a hotel, and not tell his parents that he is back.

On the train to New York, Holden meets the mother of one of his fellow Pencey students. Though he thinks this student is a complete "bastard," he tells the woman made-up stories about how shy her son is and how well respected he is at school. When he arrives at Penn Station, he goes into a phone booth and considers calling several people, but for various reasons he decides against it. He gets in a cab and asks the cab driver where the ducks in Central Park go when the lagoon freezes, but his question annoys the driver. Holden has the cab driver take him to the Edmont Hotel, where he checks himself in.

From his room at the Edmont, Holden can see into the rooms of some of the guests in the opposite wing. He observes a man putting on silk stockings, high heels, a bra, a corset, and an evening gown. He also sees a man and a woman in another room taking turns spitting mouthfuls of their drinks into each other's faces and laughing hysterically. He interprets the couple's behavior as a form of sexual play and is both upset and aroused by it. After smoking a couple of cigarettes, he calls Faith Cavendish, a woman he has never met but whose number he got from an acquaintance at Princeton. Holden thinks he remembers hearing that she used to be a stripper, and he believes he can persuade her to have sex with him. He calls her, and though she is at first annoyed to be called at such a late hour by a complete stranger, she eventually suggests that they meet the next day. Holden doesn't want to wait that long and winds up hanging up without arranging a meeting.

Holden goes downstairs to the Lavender Room and sits at a table, but the waiter realizes he's a minor and refuses to serve him. He flirts with three women in their thirties, who seem like they're from out of town and are mostly interested in catching a glimpse of a celebrity. Nevertheless, Holden dances with them and feels that he is "half in love" with the blonde one after seeing how well she dances. After making some wisecracks about his age, they leave, letting him pay their entire tab.

As Holden goes out to the lobby, he starts to think about Jane Gallagher and, in a flashback, recounts how he got to know her. They met while spending a summer vacation in Maine, played golf and checkers, and held hands at the movies. One afternoon, during a game of checkers, her stepfather came onto the porch where they were playing, and when he left Jane began to cry. Holden had moved to sit beside her and kissed her all over her face, but she wouldn't let him kiss her on the mouth. That was the closest they came to "necking."

Holden leaves the Edmont and takes a cab to Ernie's jazz club in Greenwich Village. Again, he asks the cab driver where the ducks in Central Park go in the winter, and this cabbie is even more irritable than the first one. Holden sits alone at a table in Ernie's and observes the other patrons with distaste. He runs into Lillian Simmons, one of his older brother's former girlfriends, who invites him to sit with her and her date. Holden says he has to meet someone, leaves, and walks back to the Edmont.

Maurice, the elevator operator at the Edmont, offers to send a prostitute to Holden's room for five dollars, and Holden agrees. A young woman, identifying herself as "Sunny," arrives at his door. She pulls off her dress, but Holden starts to feel "peculiar" and tries to make conversation with her. He claims that he recently underwent a spinal operation and isn't sufficiently recovered to have sex with her, but he offers to pay her anyway. She sits on his lap and talks dirty to him, but he insists on paying her five dollars and showing her the door. Sunny returns with Maurice, who demands another five dollars from Holden. When Holden refuses to pay, Maurice punches him in the stomach and leaves him on the floor, while Sunny takes five dollars from his wallet. Holden goes to bed.

He wakes up at ten o'clock on Sunday and calls Sally Hayes, an attractive girl whom he has dated in the past. They arrange to meet for a matinee showing of a Broadway play. He eats breakfast at a sandwich bar, where he converses with two nuns about Romeo and Juliet. He gives the nuns ten dollars. He tries to telephone Jane Gallagher, but her mother answers the phone, and he hangs up. He takes a cab to Central Park to look for his younger sister, Phoebe, but she isn't there. He helps one of Phoebe's schoolmates tighten her skate, and the girl tells him that Phoebe might be in the Museum of Natural History. Though he knows that Phoebe's class wouldn't be at the museum on a Sunday, he goes there anyway, but when he gets there he decides not to go in and instead takes a cab to the Biltmore Hotel to meet Sally.

Holden and Sally go to the play, and Holden is annoyed that Sally talks with a boy she knows from Andover afterward. At Sally's suggestion, they go to Radio City to ice skate. They both skate poorly and decide to get a table instead. Holden tries to explain to Sally why he is unhappy at school, and actually urges her to run away with him to Massachusetts or Vermont and live in a cabin. When she refuses, he calls her a "pain in the ass" and laughs at her when she reacts angrily. She refuses to listen to his apologies and leaves.

Holden calls Jane again, but there is no answer. He calls Carl Luce, a young man who had been Holden's student advisor at the Whooton School and who is now a student at Columbia University. Luce arranges to meet him for a drink after dinner, and Holden goes to a movie at Radio City to kill time. Holden and Luce meet at the Wicker Bar in the Seton Hotel. At Whooton, Luce had spoken frankly with some of the boys about sex, and Holden tries to draw him into a conversation about it once more. Luce grows irritated by Holden's juvenile remarks about homosexuals and about Luce's Chinese girlfriend, and he makes an excuse to leave early. Holden continues to drink Scotch and listen to the pianist and singer.

Quite drunk, Holden telephones Sally Hayes and babbles about their Christmas Eve plans. Then he goes to the lagoon in Central Park, where he used to watch the ducks as a child. It takes him a long time to find it, and by the time he does, he is freezing cold. He then decides to sneak into his own apartment building and wake his sister, Phoebe. He is forced to admit to Phoebe that he was kicked out of school, which makes her mad at him. When he tries to explain why he hates school, she accuses him of not liking anything. He tells her his fantasy of being "the catcher in the rye," a person who catches little children as they are about to fall off of a cliff. Phoebe tells him that he has misremembered the poem that he took the image from: Robert Burns's poem says "if a body meet a body, coming through the rye," not "catch a body."

Holden calls his former English teacher, Mr. Antolini, who tells Holden he can come to his apartment. Mr. Antolini asks Holden about his expulsion and tries to counsel him about his future. Holden can't hide his sleepiness, and Mr. Antolini puts him to bed on the couch. Holden awakens to find Mr. Antolini stroking his forehead. Thinking that Mr. Antolini is making a homosexual overture, Holden hastily excuses himself and leaves, sleeping for a few hours on a bench at Grand Central Station.

Holden goes to Phoebe's school and sends her a note saying that he is leaving home for good and that she should meet him at lunchtime at the museum. When Phoebe arrives, she is carrying a suitcase full of clothes, and she asks Holden to take her with him. He refuses angrily, and she cries and then refuses to speak to him. Knowing she will follow him, he walks to the zoo, and then takes her across the park to a carousel. He buys her a ticket and watches her ride it. It starts to rain heavily, but Holden is so happy watching his sister ride the carousel that he is close to tears.

Holden ends his narrative here, telling the reader that he is not going to tell the story of how he went home and got "sick." He plans to go to a new school in the fall and is cautiously optimistic about his future.

# CHARACTER LIST

*Holden Caulfield* The protagonist and narrator of the novel, Holden is a sixteen-year-old junior who has just been expelled for academic failure from a school called Pencey Prep. Although he is intelligent and sensitive, Holden narrates in a cynical and jaded voice. He finds the hypocrisy and ugliness of the world around him almost unbearable, and through his cynicism he tries to protect himself from the pain and disappointment of the adult world. However, the criticisms that Holden aims at people around him are also aimed at himself. He is uncomfortable with his own weaknesses, and at times displays as much phoniness, meanness, and superficiality as anyone else in the book. As the novel opens, Holden stands poised on the cliff separating childhood from adulthood. His inability to successfully negotiate the chasm leaves him on the verge of emotional collapse.

*Ackley* Holden's next-door neighbor in his dorm at Pencey Prep. Ackley is a pimply, insecure boy with terrible dental hygiene. He often barges into Holden's room and acts completely oblivious to Holden's hints that he should leave. Holden believes that Ackley makes up elaborate lies about his sexual experience.

*Stradlater* Holden's roommate at Pencey Prep. Stradlater is handsome, self-satisfied, and popular, but Holden calls him a "secret slob," because he appears well groomed, but his toiletries, such as his razor, are disgustingly unclean. Stradlater is sexually active and quite experienced for a prep school student, which is why Holden also calls him a "sexy bastard."

*Jane Gallagher* A girl with whom Holden spent a lot of time one summer, when their families stayed in neighboring summer houses in Maine. Jane never actually appears in *The Catcher in the Rye*, but she is extremely important to Holden, because she is one of the few girls whom he both respects and finds attractive.

*Phoebe Caulfield*  Phoebe is Holden's ten-year-old sister, whom he loves dearly. Although she is six years younger than Holden, she listens to what he says and understands him more than most other people do. Phoebe is intelligent, neat, and a wonderful dancer, and her childish innocence is one of Holden's only consistent sources of happiness throughout the novel. At times, she exhibits great maturity and even chastises Holden for his immaturity. Like Mr. Antolini, Phoebe seems to recognize that Holden is his own worst enemy.

*Allie Caulfield*  Holden's younger brother. Allie dies of leukemia three years before the start of the novel. Allie was a brilliant, friendly, red-headed boy—according to Holden, he was the smartest of the Caulfields. Holden is tormented by Allie's death and carries around a baseball glove on which Allie used to write poems in green ink.

*D. B. Caulfield*  Holden's older brother. D. B. wrote a volume of short stories that Holden admires very much, but Holden feels that D. B. prostitutes his talents by writing for Hollywood movies.

*Sally Hayes*  A very attractive girl whom Holden has known and dated for a long time. Though Sally is well read, Holden claims that she is "stupid," although it is difficult to tell whether this judgment is based in reality or merely in Holden's ambivalence about being sexually attracted to her. She is certainly more conventional than Holden in her tastes and manners.

*Mr. Spencer*  Holden's history teacher at Pencey Prep, who unsuccessfully tries to shake Holden out of his academic apathy.

*Carl Luce*   A student at Columbia who was Holden's student
advisor at the Whooton School. Luce is three
years older than Holden and has a great deal of
sexual experience. At Whooton, he was a source
of knowledge about sex for the younger boys, and
Holden tries to get him to talk about sex at their
meeting.

*Mr. Antolini*   Holden's former English teacher at the Elkton
Hills School. Mr. Antolini now teaches at New York
University. He is young, clever, sympathetic, and
likable, and Holden respects him. Holden sometimes
finds him a bit too clever, but he looks to him for
guidance. Like many characters in the novel, he drinks
heavily.

*Maurice*   The elevator operator at the Edmont Hotel, who
procures a prostitute for Holden.

*Sunny*   The prostitute whom Holden hires through Maurice.
She is one of a number of women in the book with
whom Holden clumsily attempts to connect.

# ANALYSIS OF MAJOR CHARACTERS

## HOLDEN CAULFIELD

The number of readers who have been able to identify with Holden and make him their hero is truly staggering. Something about his discontent, and his vivid way of expressing it, makes him resonate powerfully with readers who come from backgrounds completely different from his. It is tempting to inhabit his point of view and revel in his cantankerousness rather than try to deduce what is wrong with him. The obvious signs that Holden is a troubled and unreliable narrator are manifold: he fails out of four schools; he manifests complete apathy toward his future; he is hospitalized, and visited by a psychoanalyst, for an unspecified complaint; and he is unable to connect with other people. We know of two traumas in his past that clearly have something to do with his emotional state: the death of his brother Allie and the suicide of one of his schoolmates. But, even with that knowledge, Holden's peculiarities cannot simply be explained away as symptoms of a readily identifiable disorder.

The most noticeable of Holden's "peculiarities" is how extremely judgmental he is of almost everything and everybody. He criticizes and philosophizes about people who are boring, people who are insecure, and, above all, people who are "phony." Holden carries this penchant for passing judgment to such an extreme that it often becomes extremely funny, such as when he speculates that people are so crass that someone will probably write "fuck you" on his tombstone. Holden applies the term "phony" not to people who are insincere but to those who are too conventional or too typical—for instance, teachers who "act like" teachers by assuming a different demeanor in class than they do in conversation, or people who dress and act like the other members of their social class. While Holden uses the label "phony" to imply that such people are superficial, his use of the term actually indicates that his own perceptions of other people are superficial. In almost every case, he rejects more complex judgments in favor of simple categorical ones.

A second facet of Holden's personality that deserves comment is his attitude toward sex. Holden is a virgin, but he is very interested in sex, and, in fact, he spends much of the novel trying to lose his virginity. He feels strongly that sex should happen between people who care deeply about and respect one another, and he is upset by the realization that sex can be casual. Stradlater's date with Jane doesn't just make him jealous; it infuriates him to think of a girl he knows well having sex with a boy she doesn't know well. Moreover, he is disturbed by the fact that he is aroused by women whom he doesn't respect or care for, like the blonde tourist he dances with in the Lavender Room, or like Sally Hayes, whom he refers to as "stupid" even as he arranges a date with her. Finally, he is disturbed by the fact that he is aroused by kinky sexual behavior—particularly behavior that isn't respectful of one's sex partner, such as spitting in one's partner's face. Although Holden refers to such behavior as "crumby," he admits that it is pretty fun, although he doesn't think that it should be.

A brief note about Holden's name: a "caul" is a membrane that covers the head of a fetus during birth. Thus, the *caul* in his name may symbolize the blindness of childhood or the inability of the child to see the complexity of the adult world. Holden's full name might be read as Hold-on Caul-field: he wants to hold on to what he sees as his innocence, which is really his blindness.

## PHOEBE CAULFIELD

Before we meet Phoebe, Holden's side of the story is all we've been given. He implies that he is the only noble character in a world of superficial and phony adults, and we must take him at his word. There seems to be a simple dichotomy between the sweet world of childhood innocence, where Holden wants to stay, and the cruel world of shallow adult hypocrisy, where he's afraid to go. But Phoebe complicates his narrative. Instead of sympathizing with Holden's refusal to grow up, she becomes angry with him. Despite being six years younger than her brother, Phoebe understands that growing up is a necessary process; she also understands that Holden's refusal to mature reveals less about the outside world than it does about himself. Next to Phoebe, Holden's stunted emotional maturity and stubborn outlook seem less charming and more foolish. Phoebe, then, serves as a guide and surrogate for the audience. Because she knows her brother better than we do, we trust her judgments about him. Our allegiance to the narrator weakens slightly once we hear her side of the story.

Phoebe makes Holden's picture of childhood—of children romping through a field of rye—seem oversimplified, an idealized fantasy. Phoebe's character challenges Holden's view of the world: she is a child, but she does not fit into Holden's romanticized vision of child-like innocence. Although she never explicitly states it, Phoebe seems to realize that Holden's bitterness toward the rest of the world is really bitterness toward himself. She sees that he is a deeply sad, insecure young man who needs love and support. At the end of the book, when she shows up at the museum and demands to come with him, she seems not so much to need Holden as to understand that he needs her.

## MR. ANTOLINI

Mr. Antolini is the adult who comes closest to reaching Holden. He manages to avoid alienating Holden, and being labeled a "phony," because he doesn't behave conventionally. He doesn't speak to Holden in the persona of a teacher or an authority figure, as Mr. Spencer does. He doesn't object to Holden's calling him in the middle of the night or to Holden's being drunk or smoking. Moreover, by opening his door to Holden on the spur of the moment, he shows no reservations about exposing his private self, with his messy apartment, his older wife with her hair in curlers, and his own heavy drinking.

Mr. Antolini's advice to Holden about why he should apply himself to his studies is also unconventional. He recognizes that Holden is different from other students, and he validates Holden's suffering and confusion by suggesting that one day they may be worth writing about. He represents education not as a path of conformity but as a means for Holden to develop his unique voice and to find the ideas that are most appropriate to him.

When Mr. Antolini touches Holden's forehead as he sleeps, he may overstep a boundary in his display of concern and affection. However, there is little evidence to suggest that he is making a sexual overture, as Holden thinks, and much evidence that Holden misinterprets his action. Holden indicates in Chapter 19 that he is extremely nervous around possible homosexuals and that he worries about suddenly becoming one. We also know that he has been thinking about sex constantly since leaving Pencey. Finally, this is not the

CHARACTER ANALYSIS

only scene in which Holden recoils from a physical approach. He is made very uncomfortable when Sunny pulls off her dress and sits in his lap. Even when his beloved sister puts her arms around him, he remarks that she may be a little too affectionate sometimes.

Holden regrets his hasty judgment of Mr. Antolini, but this mistake is very important to him, because he finally starts to question his own practice of making snap judgments about people. Holden realizes that even if Mr. Antolini is gay, he can't simply be dismissed as a "flit," since he has also been kind and generous. Holden begins to acknowledge that Mr. Antolini is complex and that he has feelings.

# THEMES, MOTIFS & SYMBOLS

## THEMES

*Themes are the fundamental and often universal ideas explored in a literary work.*

### ALIENATION AS A FORM OF SELF-PROTECTION

Throughout the novel, Holden seems to be excluded from and victimized by the world around him. As he says to Mr. Spencer, he feels trapped on "the other side" of life, and he continually attempts to find his way in a world in which he feels he doesn't belong.

As the novel progresses, we begin to perceive that Holden's alienation is his way of protecting himself. Just as he wears his hunting hat (see "Symbols," below) to advertise his uniqueness, he uses his isolation as proof that he is better than everyone else around him and therefore above interacting with them. The truth is that interactions with other people usually confuse and overwhelm him, and his cynical sense of superiority serves as a type of self-protection. Thus, Holden's alienation is the source of what little stability he has in his life.

As readers, we can see that Holden's alienation is the cause of most of his pain. He never addresses his own emotions directly, nor does he attempt to discover the source of his troubles. He desperately needs human contact and love, but his protective wall of bitterness prevents him from looking for such interaction. Alienation is both the source of Holden's strength and the source of his problems. For example, his loneliness propels him into his date with Sally Hayes, but his need for isolation causes him to insult her and drive her away. Similarly, he longs for the meaningful connection he once had with Jane Gallagher, but he is too frightened to make any real effort to contact her. He depends upon his alienation, but it destroys him.

### THE PAINFULNESS OF GROWING UP

According to most analyses, *The Catcher in the Rye* is a bildungsroman, a novel about a young character's growth into maturity. While it is appropriate to discuss the novel in such terms, Holden Caulfield is an unusual protagonist for a bildungsroman because his central goal is to resist the process of maturity itself. As his thoughts about the Museum of Natural History demonstrate, Holden fears change and is overwhelmed by complexity. He wants everything to be easily understandable and eternally fixed, like the statues of Eskimos and Indians in the museum. He is frightened because he is guilty of the sins he criticizes in others, and because he can't understand everything around him. But he refuses to acknowledge this fear, expressing it only in a few instances—for example, when he talks about sex and admits that "[s]ex is something I just don't understand. I swear to God I don't" (Chapter 9).

Instead of acknowledging that adulthood scares and mystifies him, Holden invents a fantasy that adulthood is a world of superficiality and hypocrisy ("phoniness"), while childhood is a world of innocence, curiosity, and honesty. Nothing reveals his image of these two worlds better than his fantasy about the catcher in the rye: he imagines childhood as an idyllic field of rye in which children romp and play; adulthood, for the children of this world, is equivalent to death—a fatal fall over the edge of a cliff. His created understandings of childhood and adulthood allow Holden to cut himself off from the world by covering himself with a protective armor of cynicism. But as the book progresses, Holden's experiences, particularly his encounters with Mr. Antolini and Phoebe, reveal the shallowness of his conceptions.

### THE PHONINESS OF THE ADULT WORLD

"Phoniness," which is probably the most famous phrase from *The Catcher in the Rye*, is one of Holden's favorite concepts. It is his catch-all for describing the superficiality, hypocrisy, pretension, and shallowness that he encounters in the world around him. In Chapter 22, just before he reveals his fantasy of the catcher in the rye, Holden explains that adults are inevitably phonies, and, what's worse, they can't see their own phoniness. Phoniness, for Holden, stands as an emblem of everything that's wrong in the world around him and provides an excuse for him to withdraw into his cynical isolation.

Though oversimplified, Holden's observations are not entirely inaccurate. He can be a highly insightful narrator, and he is very aware of superficial behavior in those around him. Throughout the novel he encounters many characters who do seem affected, pretentious, or superficial—Sally Hayes, Carl Luce, Maurice and Sunny, and even Mr. Spencer stand out as examples. Some characters, like

Maurice and Sunny, are genuinely harmful. But although Holden expends so much energy searching for phoniness in others, he never directly observes his own phoniness. His deceptions are generally pointless and cruel and he notes that he is a compulsive liar. For example, on the train to New York, he perpetrates a mean-spirited and needless prank on Mrs. Morrow. He'd like us to believe that he is a paragon of virtue in a world of phoniness, but that simply isn't the case. Although he'd like to believe that the world is a simple place, and that virtue and innocence rest on one side of the fence while superficiality and phoniness rest on the other, Holden is his own counterevidence. The world is not as simple as he'd like—and needs—it to be; even he cannot adhere to the same black-and-white standards with which he judges other people.

## MOTIFS

*Motifs are recurring structures, contrasts, and literary devices that can help to develop and inform the text's major themes.*

### LONELINESS

Holden's loneliness, a more concrete manifestation of his alienation problem, is a driving force throughout the book. Most of the novel describes his almost manic quest for companionship as he flits from one meaningless encounter to another. Yet, while his behavior indicates his loneliness, Holden consistently shies away from introspection and thus doesn't really know why he keeps behaving as he does. Because Holden depends on his isolation to preserve his detachment from the world and to maintain a level of self-protection, he often sabotages his own attempts to end his loneliness. For example, his conversation with Carl Luce and his date with Sally Hayes are made unbearable by his rude behavior. His calls to Jane Gallagher are aborted for a similar reason: to protect his precious and fragile sense of individuality. Loneliness is the emotional manifestation of the alienation Holden experiences; it is both a source of great pain and a source of his security.

### RELATIONSHIPS, INTIMACY, AND SEXUALITY

Relationships, intimacy, and sexuality are also recurring motifs relating to the larger theme of alienation. Both physical and emotional relationships offer Holden opportunity to break out of his isolated shell. They also represent what he fears most about the adult world: complexity, unpredictability, and potential for conflict and change. As he demonstrates at the Museum of Natural History, Holden likes the world to be silent and frozen, predictable and unchanging. As he watches Phoebe sleep, Holden projects his own idealizations of childhood onto her. But in real-world relationships, people talk back, and Phoebe reveals how different her childhood is from Holden's romanticized notion. Because people are unpredictable, they challenge Holden and force him to question his senses of self-confidence and self-worth. For intricate and unspoken reasons, seemingly stemming from Allie's death, Holden has trouble dealing with this kind of complexity. As a result, he has isolated himself and fears intimacy. Although he encounters opportunities for both physical and emotional intimacy, he bungles them all, wrapping himself in a psychological armor of critical cynicism and bitterness. Even so, Holden desperately continues searching for new relationships, always undoing himself only at the last moment.

### LYING AND DECEPTION

Lying and deception are the most obvious and hurtful elements of the larger category of phoniness. Holden's definition of phoniness relies mostly on a kind of self-deception: he seems to reserve the most scorn for people who think that they are something they are not or who refuse to acknowledge their own weaknesses. But lying to others is also a kind of phoniness, a type of deception that indicates insensitivity, callousness, or even cruelty. Of course, Holden himself is guilty of both these crimes. His random and repeated lying highlights his own self-deception—he refuses to acknowledge his own shortcomings and is unwilling to consider how his behavior affects those around him. Through his lying and deception, Holden proves that he is just as guilty of phoniness as the people he criticizes.

## SYMBOLS

> *Symbols are objects, characters, figures, and colors used to represent abstract ideas or concepts.*

### THE "CATCHER IN THE RYE"

As the source of the book's title, this symbol merits close inspection. It first appears in Chapter 16, when a kid Holden admires for walking in the street rather than on the sidewalk is singing the Robert Burns song "Comin' Thro' the Rye." In Chapter 22, when Phoebe asks Holden what he wants to do with his life, he replies with his image, from the song, of a "catcher in the rye." Holden imagines a field of rye perched high on a cliff, full of children romping and playing. He says he would like to protect the children from falling off the edge of the cliff by "catching" them if they were on the verge of tumbling over. As Phoebe points out, Holden has misheard the lyric. He thinks the line is "If a body catch a body comin' through the rye," but the actual lyric is "If a body meet a body, coming through the rye."

The song "Comin' Thro' the Rye" asks if it is wrong for two people to have a romantic encounter out in the fields, away from the public eye, even if they don't plan to have a commitment to one another. It is highly ironic that the word "meet" refers to an encounter that leads to recreational sex, because the word that Holden substitutes—"catch"—takes on the exact opposite meaning in his mind. Holden wants to catch children before they fall out of innocence into knowledge of the adult world, including knowledge of sex.

## HOLDEN'S RED HUNTING HAT

The red hunting hat is one of the most recognizable symbols from twentieth-century American literature. It is inseparable from our image of Holden, with good reason: it is a symbol of his uniqueness and individuality. The hat is outlandish, and it shows that Holden desires to be different from everyone around him. At the same time, he is very self-conscious about the hat—he always mentions when he is wearing it, and he often doesn't wear it if he is going to be around people he knows. The presence of the hat, therefore, mirrors the central conflict in the book: Holden's need for isolation versus his need for companionship.

It is worth noting that the hat's color, red, is the same as that of Allie's and Phoebe's hair. Perhaps Holden associates it with the innocence and purity he believes these characters represent and wears it as a way to connect to them. He never explicitly comments on the hat's significance other than to mention its unusual appearance.

## THE MUSEUM OF NATURAL HISTORY

Holden tells us the symbolic meaning of the museum's displays: they appeal to him because they are frozen and unchanging. He also mentions that he is troubled by the fact that he has changed every time he returns to them. The museum represents the world Holden wishes he could live in: it's the world of his "catcher in the rye" fantasy, a world where nothing ever changes, where everything is simple, understandable, and infinite. Holden is terrified by the unpredictable challenges of the world—he hates conflict, he is confused by Allie's senseless death, and he fears interaction with other people.

## THE DUCKS IN THE CENTRAL PARK LAGOON

Holden's curiosity about where the ducks go during the winter reveals a genuine, more youthful side to his character. For most of the book, he sounds like a grumpy old man who is angry at the world, but his search for the ducks represents the curiosity of youth and a joyful willingness to encounter the mysteries of the world. It is a memorable moment, because Holden clearly lacks such willingness in other aspects of his life.

The ducks and their pond are symbolic in several ways. Their mysterious perseverance in the face of an inhospitable environment resonates with Holden's understanding of his own situation. In addition, the ducks prove that some vanishings are only temporary. Traumatized and made acutely aware of the fragility of life by his brother Allie's death, Holden is terrified by the idea of change and disappearance. The ducks vanish every winter, but they return every spring, thus symbolizing change that isn't permanent, but cyclical. Finally, the pond itself becomes a minor metaphor for the world as Holden sees it, because it is "partly frozen and partly not frozen." The pond is in transition between two states, just as Holden is in transition between childhood and adulthood.

SYMBOLS

# Summary & Analysis

## Chapters 1–2

### Summary: Chapter 1

Holden Caulfield writes his story from a rest home to which he has been sent for therapy. He refuses to talk about his early life, mentioning only that his brother D. B. is a Hollywood writer. He hints that he is bitter because D. B. has sold out to Hollywood, forsaking a career in serious literature for the wealth and fame of the movies. He then begins to tell the story of his breakdown, beginning with his departure from Pencey Prep, a famous school he attended in Agerstown, Pennsylvania.

Holden's career at Pencey Prep has been marred by his refusal to apply himself, and after failing four of his five subjects—he passed only English—he has been forbidden to return to the school after the fall term. The Saturday before Christmas vacation begins, Holden stands on Thomsen Hill overlooking the football field, where Pencey plays its annual grudge match against Saxon Hall. Holden has no interest in the game and hadn't planned to watch it at all. He is the manager of the school's fencing team and is supposed to be in New York for a meet, but he lost the team's equipment on the subway, forcing everyone to return early.

Holden is full of contempt for the prep school, but he looks for a way to "say goodbye" to it. He fondly remembers throwing a football with friends even after it grew dark outside. Holden walks away from the game to go say goodbye to Mr. Spencer, a former history teacher who is very old and ill with the flu. He sprints to Spencer's house, but since he is a heavy smoker, he has to stop to catch his breath at the main gate. At the door, Spencer's wife greets Holden warmly, and he goes in to see his teacher.

### Summary: Chapter 2

> "Life is a game, boy. Life is a game that one plays
> according to the rules."
>
> (See QUOTATIONS, p. 51)

Holden greets Mr. Spencer and his wife in a manner that suggests he is close to them. He is put off by his teacher's rather decrepit condition but seems otherwise to respect him. In his sickroom, Spencer tries to lecture Holden about his academic failures. He confirms Pencey's headmaster's assertion that "[l]ife is a game" and tells Holden that he must learn to play by the rules. Although Spencer clearly feels affection for Holden, he bluntly reminds the boy that he flunked him, and even forces him to listen to the terrible essay he handed in about the ancient Egyptians. Finally, Spencer tries to convince Holden to think about his future. Not wanting to be lectured, Holden interrupts Spencer and leaves, returning to his dorm room before dinner.

---

ANALYSIS: CHAPTERS 1–2

Holden Caulfield is the protagonist of *The Catcher in the Rye,* and the most important function of these early chapters is to establish the basics of his personality. From the beginning of the novel, Holden tells his story in a bitterly cynical voice. He refuses to discuss his early life, he says, because he is bored by "all that David Copperfield kind of crap." He gives us a hint that something catastrophic has happened in his life, acknowledging that he writes from a rest home to tell about "this madman stuff" that happened to him around the previous Christmas, but he doesn't yet go into specifics. The particularities of his story are in keeping with his cynicism and his boredom. He has failed out of school, and he leaves Spencer's house abruptly because he does not enjoy being confronted by his actions.

Beneath the surface of Holden's tone and behavior runs a more idealistic, emotional current. He begins the story of his last day at Pencey Prep by telling how he stood at the top of Thomsen Hill, preparing to leave the school and trying to feel "some kind of a goodby." He visits Spencer in Chapter 2 even though he failed Spencer's history class, and he seems to respond to Mrs. Spencer's kindness. What bothers him the most, in these chapters and throughout the book, is the hypocrisy and ugliness around him, which diminish the innocence and beauty of the external world—the unpleasantness of Spencer's sickroom, for instance, and his hairless legs sticking out of his pajamas. Salinger thus treats his narrator as more than a mere portrait of a cynical postwar rich kid at an impersonal and pressure-filled boarding school. Even in these early chapters, Holden connects with life on a very idealistic level; he seems to feel its flaws so deeply that he tries to shield himself with a veneer of cynicism. *The Catcher in the Rye* is in many ways a book about the betrayal of innocence by the modern world; despite his bitter tone, Holden is an innocent searching desperately for a way to connect with the world around him that will not cause him pain. In these early chapters, the reader already begins to sense that Holden is not an entirely reliable narrator and that the reality of his situation is somehow different from the way he describes it. In part this is simply because Holden is a first-person narrator describing his own experiences from his own point of view. Any individual's point of view, in any novel or story, is necessarily limited. The reader never forgets for a moment who is telling this story, because the tone, grammar, and diction are consistently those of an adolescent—albeit a highly intelligent and expressive one—and every event receives Holden's distinctive commentary. However, Holden's narrative contains inconsistencies that make us question what he says. For instance, Holden characterizes Spencer's behavior throughout as vindictive and mean-spirited, but Spencer's actions clearly seem to be motivated by concern for Holden's well-being. Holden seems to be looking for reasons not to listen to Spencer.

## CHAPTERS 3–4

### SUMMARY: CHAPTER 3

> *"This is a people shooting hat," I said. "I shoot people in this hat."*
>
> *(See* QUOTATIONS, *p. 52)*

Holden lives in Ossenburger Hall, which is named after a wealthy Pencey graduate who made a fortune in the discount funeral home business. In his room, Holden sits and reads Isak Dinesen's *Out of Africa* while wearing his new hunting hat, a flamboyant red cap with a long peaked brim and earflaps. He is interrupted by Ackley, a pimply student who lives next door. According to Holden, Ackley is a supremely irritating classmate who constantly barges into the room, exhibits disgusting personal habits and poor hygiene, and always acts as if he's doing others a favor by spending time with them. Ackley does not seem to have many friends. He prevents Holden from reading by puttering around the room and pestering him with annoying questions. Ackley further aggravates Holden by cutting his fingernails on the floor, despite Holden's repeated requests that he stop. He refuses to take Holden's hints that he ought to leave. When Holden's handsome and popular roommate, Stradlater, enters, Ackley, who hates Stradlater, quickly returns to his own room. Stradlater mentions that he has a date waiting for him but wants to shave.

### SUMMARY: CHAPTER 4

Holden goes to the bathroom with Stradlater and talks to him while he shaves. Holden contrasts Stradlater's personal habits with Ackley's: whereas Ackley is ugly and has poor dental hygiene, Stradlater is outwardly attractive but does not keep his razor or other toiletries clean. He decides that while Ackley is an obvious slob, Stradlater is a "secret slob." The two joke around, then Stradlater asks Holden to write an English composition for him, because his date won't leave him with time to do it on his own. Holden asks about the date and learns that Stradlater is taking out a girl Holden knows, Jane Gallagher. (Stradlater carelessly calls her "Jean.") Holden clearly has strong feelings for Jane and remembers her vividly. He tells Stradlater that when she played checkers, she used to keep all of her kings in the back row because she liked the way they looked there. Stradlater is uninterested. Holden is displeased that Stradlater, one of the few sexually experienced boys at Pencey, is taking Jane on a date. He wants to say hello to her while she waits for Stradlater, but decides he isn't in the mood. Before he leaves for his date, Stradlater borrows Holden's hound's-tooth jacket.

After Stradlater leaves, Holden is tormented by thoughts of Jane and Stradlater. Ackley barges in again and sits in Holden's room, squeezing pimples until dinnertime.

---

### ANALYSIS: CHAPTERS 3–4

These chapters establish the way Holden interacts with his peers. Holden despises "phonies"—people whose surface behavior distorts or disguises their inner feelings. Even his brother D. B. incurs his displeasure by accepting a big paycheck to write for the movies; Holden considers the movies to be the phoniest of the phony and emphasizes throughout the book the loathing he has for Hollywood.

Unfortunately, Holden is surrounded by phonies in his circa-prep school. Preening Ackley and self-absorbed Stradlater act as his immediate contrasts. But, despite their flaws, he acts with basic kindness toward them, agreeing to write Stradlater's English composition for him in Chapter 4, even though Stradlater is out with

Jane Gallagher, a girl Holden seems to care for very deeply. The pressure of adolescent sexuality—an important theme throughout *The Catcher in the Rye*—makes itself felt here for the first time: Holden's greatest worry is that Stradlater will make sexual advances toward Jane.

Stradlater and Ackley sound like appallingly unsympathetic characters, but this is completely the result of the tone in which Holden describes them. For instance, Holden indicates his awareness that Ackley behaves in annoying ways because he is insecure and unpopular, but instead of trying to imagine what Ackley wants or why he does things, he focuses on Ackley's surface—literally, his skin. By describing in minute detail Ackley's nail trimming and pimple squeezing, Holden makes him seem disgusting and subhuman.

Holden's interactions also reveal how lonely he is. He describes Ackley as isolated and ostracized, but it's easy to see the parallel between Ackley's and Holden's situations. Holden notes that he and Ackley are the only two guys not at the football game. Both are isolated, and both maintain a bitter, critical exterior in order to shield themselves from the world that assaults them. In Ackley especially, we can see the cruelty of the situation. Ackley's isolation is perpetuated by his annoying habits, but his annoying habits protect him from the dangers of interaction and intimacy. Ackley's situation greatly illuminates Holden's own inner landscape: intimacy and interaction are what he needs and fears most.

Holden's new hunting hat, with its funny earflaps, becomes very important to him. Throughout the novel, it serves as a kind of protective device, which Holden uses for more than physical warmth and comfort. When he wears the hat, he always claims not to care what people think about his appearance, which might be a source of self-conscious embarrassment for Holden—he is extremely tall for his age, very thin, and, though he is only sixteen, has a great deal of gray hair. But it is also important to note when Holden does not wear the hat. Part of him seems to want to display his rebelliousness, but another part of him wants to fit in—or, at least, to hide his unique personality. Although he mentions the freezing temperature, Holden does not wear the hat near the football game or at Spencer's house; he waits for the privacy of his own room to put it on.

## CHAPTERS 5–6

### SUMMARY: CHAPTER 5

After a dry and unappetizing steak dinner in the dining hall, Holden gets into a snowball fight with some of the other Pencey boys. He and his friend Mal Brossard decide to take a bus into Agerstown to see a movie—though Holden hates movies—and Holden convinces Mal to let Ackley go with them. As it turns out, Ackley and Brossard have already seen the film, so the trio simply eats some burgers, plays a little pinball, and heads back to Pencey.

After the excursion, Mal goes off to look for a bridge game, and Ackley sits on Holden's bed squeezing pimples and concocting stories about a girl he claims to have had sex with the summer before. Holden finally gets him to leave by beginning to work on the English assignment for Stradlater. Stradlater had said the composition was supposed to be a simple description of a room, a house, or something similarly straightforward. But Holden cannot think of anything to say about a house or a room, so he writes about a baseball glove that his brother Allie used to copy poems onto in green ink.

Several years before, Allie died of leukemia. Though he was two years younger than Holden, Holden says that Allie was the most intelligent member of his family. He also says that Allie was an incredibly nice, innocent child. Holden clearly still feels Allie's loss strongly. He gives a brief description of Allie, mentioning his bright red hair. He also recounts that the night Allie died, he slept in the garage and broke all the windows with his bare hands. After he finishes the composition for Stradlater, he stares out the window and listens to Ackley snore in the next room.

### SUMMARY: CHAPTER 6

Home from his date, Stradlater barges into the room. He reads Holden's composition and becomes visibly annoyed, asserting that it has nothing to do with the assignment and that it's no wonder Holden is being expelled. Holden tears the composition up and throws it away angrily. Afterward, he smokes a cigarette in the room just to annoy Stradlater. The tension between the two increases when Holden asks Stradlater about his date with Jane. When Stradlater nonchalantly refuses to tell Holden any of the details, Holden attacks him, but Stradlater pins him to the floor and tries to get him to calm down. Holden relentlessly insults Stradlater, driving

him crazy until he punches Holden and bloodies his nose. Stradlater then becomes worried that he has hurt Holden and will get
into trouble. Holden insults him some more, and Stradlater finally
leaves the room. Holden gets up and goes into Ackley's room, his
face covered in blood.

## ANALYSIS: CHAPTERS 5–6

Holden's kindness to Ackley in Chapter 5 comes as a surprise after
the disdain that Holden has displayed for him in the previous two
chapters. Though he continues to complain about Ackley, the sympathy he feels for his next-door neighbor is evident when he convinces Mal Brossard to let Ackley join them at the movies. Equally
surprising is Holden's willingness to go to the movies after his dia-
tribes against their superficiality. Holden's actions are inconsistent
with his opinions, but instead of making him seem like a hypocrite,
this makes him more likable: he is kind to Ackley without comment-
ing on it, and he shows himself capable of going to the movies with
his friends like a normal teenager.

The most important revelation in these chapters comes about
when Holden writes the composition for Stradlater, divulging that
his brother Allie died of leukemia several years before. Holden
idealizes Allie, praising his intelligence and sensitivity—the poem-
covered baseball glove is a perfect emblem for both—but remain-
ing silent about his emotional reaction to Allie's death. He alludes
to his behavior almost in passing, saying that he slept in the garage on the night of Allie's death and broke all the windows with
his bare hands, "just for the hell of it." He tried to break the car
windows as well, but could not because his hand was already frac-
tured from smashing the garage windows. Throughout the novel,
it becomes increasingly clear that Allie's death was one of the most
traumatic experiences of Holden's life and may play a major role
in his current psychological breakdown. Indeed, the cynicism that
Holden uses to avoid expressing his feelings may result from Allie's death.

Holden seems to feel increasing pressure as he moves toward
leaving school, and Salinger manipulates the details of Holden's
physical environment to match his protagonist's feelings. Holden
cannot get a moment alone; Ackley continues to barge in with
his made-up sex stories, and when Holden writes the very personal composition about his brother Allie, Stradlater criticizes it
and then taunts Holden about Jane. When Holden finally snaps

and attacks his roommate, Stradlater easily overpowers him, and when he tries to seek refuge in Ackley's room, Ackley is so unpleasant that Holden cannot relax. He leaves abruptly, as though trying to escape the torment of his environment. What Holden does not yet realize, however, is that he carries his torment with him, inside himself.

## CHAPTERS 7–9

### SUMMARY: CHAPTER 7

Holden talks for a while with Ackley and then tries to fall asleep in the bed belonging to Ackley's roommate, who is away for the weekend. But he cannot stop imagining Jane fooling around with Stradlater, and he has trouble falling asleep. He wakes Ackley and talks with him some more, asking whether he could run off and join a monastery without being Catholic. Ackley is annoyed by the conversation, and Holden is annoyed by Ackley's "phoniness," so he leaves. Outside, in the dorm's hallway, he decides that he will leave for New York that night instead of waiting until Wednesday. After passing a few days there in secret, he will wait until his parents have digested the news of his expulsion before he returns to their apartment. He packs his bags, dons his hunting hat, and begins to cry. As he heads into the hallway, he yells "Sleep tight, ya morons!" to the boys on his floor before stepping outside to leave Pencey forever.

### SUMMARY: CHAPTER 8

Holden walks the entire way to the train station and catches a late train to New York. At Trenton, an attractive older woman gets on and sits next to him. She turns out to be the mother of his classmate, Ernest Morrow. He dislikes Ernest immensely but tells extravagant lies about him to his mother, claiming that he is the most popular boy on campus and would have been elected class president if he'd let the other boys nominate him. Holden tells her his own name is Rudolph Schmidt, which is actually the school janitor's name. When she asks why he is leaving Pencey early, Holden claims to be returning to New York for a brain tumor operation.

### SUMMARY: CHAPTER 9

At Penn Station, Holden wants to call someone but cannot think of anyone to call—his brother, D. B., is in Hollywood; his sister,

Phoebe, is young and probably asleep; he doesn't feel like calling Jane Gallagher; and another girl, Sally Hayes, has a mother who hates him. So, Holden takes a cab to the Edmont Hotel. He tries to make conversation with the driver, asking him where the ducks in the Central Park lagoon go in the winter, but the driver is uninterested. In his room at the Edmont, he looks out across the hotel courtyard into the lighted windows on the other side and discovers a variety of bizarre acts taking place. One man dresses in women's clothing, and in another room a man and a woman take turns spitting mouthfuls of their drinks into each other's face. Holden begins to feel aroused, so he calls Faith Cavendish, a promiscuous girl recommended to him by a boy he met at a party, and tries to make a date with her. She refuses, claiming she needs her beauty sleep. She offers to meet him the next day, but he doesn't want to wait that long, and he hangs up without arranging to meet her.

---

## ANALYSIS: CHAPTERS 7–9

*The Catcher in the Rye* is a chronicle of Holden Caulfield's emotional breakdown, but Holden never comments on it directly. At no point in the story does he say that he is undergoing an emotional strain; he simply describes his increasingly desperate behavior without much explanation. Salinger cleverly manipulates Holden's narrative to signal to the reader that there is more to the story than what Holden admits or describes. In the previous sections, Holden exhibited a number of behaviors that might indicate a troubled mind: running through the snow to Spencer's house, writing Stradlater's English composition about Allie's baseball glove, attacking Stradlater for joking about Jane, leaving his dorm forever in the middle of the night, and yelling an insult down the hallway on his way out. In this section, Holden's frantic loneliness and constant lying further the implication that he is not well mentally or emotionally.

As soon as he gets off the train in New York in Chapter 9, Holden wants to call someone and seems especially to want to call Jane, but he is apparently too nervous (he suspiciously claims not to "feel like it" and runs through a long list of people he could contact instead). This seems particularly strange given Holden's cynicism and evident dislike for most people; in Chapter 8, for instance, he describes enjoying the solitude of late-night train rides. His desire for human contact becomes even more intense as the section progresses:

he begins to feel sexually aroused and tries to make a date with a stranger whose number he was given at a party, then goes to a nightclub to flirt with older women. Holden's constant lying, in this section and throughout the novel, is a mark of immaturity and imbalance. As soon as he meets Mrs. Morrow on the train, Holden begins telling ridiculous lies, claiming to be named Rudolph Schmidt and to be going to New York for a brain tumor operation. He feels guilty for lying, but the only way he can stop is to stop talking altogether. There is no particular rhyme or reason for the lies he tells Mrs. Morrow—his intentions toward her may be kind, or cruel, or simply careless. What does seem clear is that he lies to deflect attention from himself and what he is doing.

In his reactions to the other guests in the hotel, whom he refers to as "perverts," Holden reveals a great deal about his attitudes toward sex and toward what makes him uncomfortable about sexuality. He admits that he is aroused by the idea of spitting in someone's face and that the couple across the courtyard seems to be having fun. But he thinks that people should only have sex if they care deeply for one another, and "crumby" behavior such as this seems disrespectful. What bothers him is his perception that sexual attraction can be separate from respect and intimacy, and that sex can be casual or kinky. He knows this from his own experience with a former girlfriend, from observing Stradlater's mating habits, and from watching his new neighbors. As he tells his story, Holden never seems particularly concerned about his own behavior or that of those around him. He often seems angry, but he rarely discusses his feelings. By combining what we know about Holden from his narration with his actions in the story, we can piece together the desperation, the pressure, and the trauma he endures during this difficult time in his life.

## CHAPTERS 10–12

### SUMMARY: CHAPTER 10

Still feeling restless, Holden changes his shirt and goes downstairs to the Lavender Room, the Edmont's nightclub. Before he leaves his room, he thinks again about calling his little sister, Phoebe. Referring to her as "old Phoebe," he gives a description of her character that is remarkably similar to the description he gave of Allie in Chapter 5. Like Allie, she has red hair and is unusually intelligent for her age. He recalls the time he and Phoebe went to see Hitchcock's *The*

*Steps* (despite his professed loathing for the cinema, he has clearly seen many movies and has strong opinions about them). He notes Phoebe's humor and cleverness, and mentions that she writes never-ending fictional stories that feature a character named "Hazle" Weatherfield. According to Holden, Phoebe's one flaw is that she is perhaps too emotional.

In the Lavender Room, Holden takes a table and tries to order a cocktail. He explains that due to his height and his gray hair, he is often able to order alcohol, but, in this case, the waiter refuses. He flirts and dances with three women who are visiting from Seattle. They seem amused but uninterested in this obviously young man who tries to appear older and debonair. After tolerating him for a while, they begin to laugh at him; they also depress him by being obsessed with movie stars. When Holden lies to one of them about having just seen Gary Cooper, she tells the other two that she caught a glimpse of Gary Cooper as well. Holden pays for their drinks, then leaves the Lavender Room.

## Summary: Chapter 11

As he walks out to the lobby, Holden reminisces about Jane. Their families' summer homes in Maine were next door to one another, and he met her after his mother confronted her mother about a Doberman pinscher that frequently relieved itself on the Caulfields' lawn. Holden and Jane became close—Jane was the only person to whom Holden ever showed Allie's baseball glove. One day, Jane's alcoholic stepfather came out to the porch where Holden and Jane were playing checkers and asked Jane for cigarettes; Jane refused to answer him, and, when he left, she began to cry. Holden held her, kissing her face and comforting her. Apart from that incident, their physical relationship was mild, but they used to hold hands constantly. When you held Jane's hand, Holden reminisces, "all you knew was, you were happy. You really were." Holden then feels suddenly upset, and he returns to his room. He notices that the lights in the "perverts'" rooms are out. He is still wide awake, so he heads downstairs and grabs a taxi.

## Summary: Chapter 12

Holden takes a cab to a Greenwich Village nightclub called Ernie's, a spot he used to frequent with D. B. His cab driver is named Horwitz, and Holden takes a liking to him. But when Holden tries to ask him about the ducks in the Central Park lagoon, Horwitz unexpectedly becomes angry. At Ernie's, Holden listens to Ernie play the piano but is unimpressed. He takes a table, drinks Scotch and soda, and listens to the conversations around him, which he finds depressing and phony. He encounters an obnoxious girl named Lillian Simmons, whom D. B. used to date, and is forced to leave the nightclub to get away from her.

---

ANALYSIS: CHAPTERS 10–12

By this point in the novel, it's clear that loneliness is at the heart of Holden's problems. When he arrives in New York, it is already quite late in the evening, but he embarks on an almost manic quest for interaction. His call to Faith Cavendish in Chapter 9 hinted at Holden's desperation—calling a girl you've never met in the middle of the night is not quite normal—but here we see the depth of Holden's feelings of loneliness and alienation.

Despite his independent nature, Holden demonstrates how badly he needs companionship. In these chapters especially, his thoughts are always of other people. He thinks about Phoebe, he repeatedly remembers Jane, and he mentally ridicules the people at surrounding tables. But Holden never mentions himself. He avoids introspection and reflection on his own shortcomings and problems by focusing on the world around him, usually through a dismissive and critical lens. His focus on other people reveals the extent to which he longs for companionship, love, and compassionate interaction to help him through a difficult period in his life.

Through his nostalgic memories of Jane, we gain insight into the type of companionship Holden wants. He mentions that he knew he was happy when he was with Jane—this is a certitude that he is lacking at the present moment. His memories of Jane are especially touching because he describes a very deep emotional connection. Additionally, their moments of intimacy were subtle and extremely personal, free of any sort of posturing or phoniness.

The key moment of Jane and Holden's relationship bears a curious resemblance to Holden's present situation. After her stepfather's intrusion, Jane is overwhelmed by a pain she cannot articulate, a deep sadness that she cannot put into words. Holden, full of silent compassion and understanding, knows what to do to help her through hard times. Now, he finds himself in a similar situation, struggling with a pain that he can't talk about with anyone in the book, including the reader. He desperately needs the same deep, compassionate connection he says he once experienced with Jane.

Holden's self-delusion and unreliability as a narrator continue to grow. When he enters the Lavender Room, he depicts himself as a wise-beyond-his-years, debonair playboy. But because the waiter refuses to serve him alcohol, and because the girls laugh at his advances, we doubt that Holden's self-description is accurate. Holden rationalizes the girls' dismissal of him by saying that they are silly tourist hicks. Although there does seem to be a bit of provincialism in their character, it's fairly clear that the girls are amused by the situation and that they indulge Holden in his flirtation out of pity combined with a touch of mockery. Holden likes to imagine that he is a mature individual who perceptively sees all the hidden details around him, but in actuality he's just a kid. Once again, Holden's inability to understand the world around him—or, perhaps, his unwillingness to acknowledge the world around him—reveals his profound disconnection and isolation.

## CHAPTERS 13–15

### SUMMARY: CHAPTER 13

Feeling like a coward for leaving Ernie's, Holden walks the forty-one blocks from the nightclub back to the hotel. Along the way, he thinks about his gloves, which were stolen at Pencey. He imagines an elaborate confrontation with the unknown thief, but he acknowledges that he is a coward at heart, afraid of violence and confrontation. When he reaches the Edmont, he takes the elevator up to his room. The elevator operator offers to send him a prostitute for five dollars, and Holden, depressed and flustered, accepts. While waiting in his room, he again thinks about his cowardice, because he feels that his lack of aggression has prevented him from ever sleeping with a woman. Women, Holden believes, want a man who asserts power and control. As he broods, the prostitute, Sunny, arrives. She is a cynical young girl with a high voice. Holden becomes flustered, especially so when she removes her dress. She sits on his lap and tries to seduce him, but he is extremely nervous and tells her he is unable to have sex because he is recovering from an operation on his "clavichord." He finally pays her the five dollars he owes and asks her to leave. She claims that the price is ten, but he refuses to pay her more, and she leaves in a huff.

## Summary: Chapter 14

Holden sits in his hotel room and smokes for a while. He remembers an incident shortly before Allie's death when he excluded Allie from a BB-gun game—he still feels guilty for having left Allie out. Eventually, he goes to bed. He feels like praying, but his distaste for organized religion prevents him from following through on his inclination. Suddenly, there is a knock at his door. In his pajamas, Holden opens the door to face the burly elevator operator, Maurice, who has returned with Sunny to collect the extra five dollars Sunny demanded. Holden tries to refuse, but Maurice pins him against a wall while Sunny takes the money from his wallet. Maurice snaps his finger into Holden's groin, and Holden starts to insult him in response. Maurice slugs Holden in the stomach and leaves him crumpled on the floor. Holden imagines himself as a movie character, taking his revenge on Maurice after having been plugged in the gut with a gangster's bullet. Finally, he manages to get into bed and go to sleep.

## Summary: Chapter 15

The next morning, Holden calls Sally Hayes and makes a date with her for later that afternoon. He checks out of the hotel and leaves his bags in a locker at Grand Central Station. He worries about losing his money and mentions that his father frequently gets angry when Holden loses things. He also describes his mother a bit, noting that she "hasn't felt too healthy since my brother Allie died." Holden worries that the news of his expulsion will particularly distress his fragile mother, for whom he seems to care a great deal.

Holden goes to eat breakfast at a little sandwich bar, where he meets two nuns who are moving to Manhattan to teach in a school. Holden thinks about the superficial money-driven world of the prep school he has just left. Then he talks to one of the nuns about Romeo and Juliet. Despite his earlier expression of distaste for organized religion, he forces them to take ten dollars as a charitable contribution. After they leave, although he realizes he needs money to pay for his date with Sally, he begins to regret having given only ten dollars. He concludes that money always makes people depressed.

---

## Analysis: Chapters 13–15

During his previous expeditions around town, Holden maintained a distance from the people he was with, dismissing them with scorn.

As a result, he was able to protect his vision of an ideal world: instead of dealing with real people and situations, he daydreams about Phoebe's innocence and Jane's warmth. Up to this point, Holden has been able to avoid a clash between his real and his ideal worlds, but in these chapters, the conflict becomes unavoidable, and Holden is caught in a moment of crisis and danger.

Sunny represents another of Holden's attempts at female companionship, but she could not be more different from the idealized Jane for whom Holden yearns. Whereas Holden's relationship with Jane brought him emotional satisfaction, his relationship with a prostitute can only be superficial, sexual, and devoid of emotion. But Jane appears only in Holden's memory, while the prostitute appears in his room. She concretizes Holden's continual conflict, representing something he both wants and doesn't want, something he needs yet fears.

The tension between Holden's growing sexuality and his fragile innocence grows much stronger throughout this section. He wants to live in a beautiful world, but the pressure of his emerging sexuality and the demands of his loneliness compel him to enter into encounters with people like Maurice and Sunny. Such encounters are so far removed from the idealized encounters he fantasizes about that he departs from them much more hurt and wounded than before. Scared of the adult world, Holden clearly shies away from intimacy and is terrified of his burgeoning sexuality: he is too scared both to call Jane and to sleep with Sunny. He takes refuge in isolation, but this isolation only deepens the pain of alienation and loneliness.

While the harm Maurice and Sunny cause Holden is obvious, there are much more subtle reasons why his encounter with the nuns leaves him feeling hurt and wounded. Holden has constructed a simplistic divide between childhood, which he sees as innocent and good, and adulthood, which he finds superficial and evil. This worldview allows him to maintain his cynical barrier of defense: he is able to rationalize his loneliness by pretending that every adult around him is phony and annoying. In a way, Holden's encounter with Maurice and Sunny helps Holden by reaffirming his understanding of a cruel and senseless adult world. But the nuns are kind, intelligent, and sympathetic. They don't conform to his stereotyped understanding of organized religion, nor do they seem to have the phoniness that Holden expects of anything institutionalized. He is surprised that one nun loves Romeo and Juliet and that they can have a conversation about it.

## CHAPTERS 16–17

### SUMMARY: CHAPTER 16

After breakfast, Holden goes for a walk. He thinks about the self-lessness of the nuns and can't imagine anyone he knows being so generous and giving. He heads down Broadway to buy a record called "Little Shirley Beans" for Phoebe. He likes the record because, although it is for children, it is sung by a black blues singer who makes it sound raunchy, not cute. He thinks about Phoebe, whom he considers to be a wonderful girl because, although she's only ten, she always understands what Holden means when he talks to her. He sees an oblivious little boy walking in the street, singing, "If a body catch a body coming through the rye." The innocence of the scene cheers him up, and he decides to call Jane, although he hangs up when her mother answers the phone. In preparation for his date with Sally, he buys theater tickets to a show called "I Know My Love," which stars the Lunts.

> The best thing, though, in that museum was that everything always stayed right where it was.
> (See QUOTATIONS, p. 53)

Holden wants to see Phoebe, and he goes to look for her in the park because he remembers that she often roller-skates there on Sundays. He meets a girl who knows Phoebe. At first, she tells him that his sister is on a school trip to the Museum of Natural History, but then she remembers that the trip was the previous day. Nevertheless, Holden walks to the museum, remembering his own class trips. He focuses on the way life is frozen in the museum's exhibits: models of Eskimos and Indians stand as though petrified and birds hang from the ceiling, seemingly in mid-flight. He remarks that every time he went to the museum, he felt that he had changed, while the museum had stayed exactly the same.

### SUMMARY: CHAPTER 17

At two o'clock, Holden goes to meet Sally at the Biltmore Hotel; she is late but looks very attractive, so he immediately forgives her tardiness. They make out in the taxi on the way to the theater. At the play, the actors annoy Holden because, like Ernie the piano player, they are almost too good at what they do and seem full of themselves. During intermission, Sally irritates Holden by flirting with a pretentious boy from Andover, another prep school, but he nonetheless agrees to take her ice-skating at "Radio City" (Radio City Music Hall is part of Rockefeller Center, where there is an ice-skating rink) after the show. While skating, Holden speculates that Sally only wanted to go ice-skating so she could wear a short skirt and show off her "cute ass," but he admits that he finds it attractive. When they take a break and sit down indoors, Holden begins to unravel. Oscillating between shouting and hushed tones, he rants about all the "phonies" at his prep schools and in New York society, and talks about how alienated he feels. He becomes even more crazy and impetuous, saying that he and Sally should run away together and escape from society, living on their own in a cabin. When she points out that his dreams are ridiculous, he becomes more and more agitated. The quarrel builds until Holden calls Sally a "royal pain in the ass," and she begins to cry. Holden starts to apologize, but Sally is upset and angry with him, and, finally, he leaves without her.

## ANALYSIS: CHAPTERS 16–17

Things go from bad to worse for Holden in these chapters. His behavior during his date with Sally is the surest sign yet that he is heading toward emotional collapse. Throughout his tirade, Sally asks Holden to stop yelling, and he claims not to have been yelling, indicating that he is unaware of his own extreme agitation. His attempt to convince a shallow socialite like Sally to run away with him to a cabin in the wilderness also shows his increasing distance from reality—or, at least, his inability to deal with the reality in which he finds himself.

Though Holden admits his behavior is odd when he says, "I swear to God I'm a madman," he doesn't do much to explain its significance. Salinger continues to drop hints—like Sally's requests for Holden to stop yelling—to signal that the story behind Holden's narration is darker and more troubling than it might at first appear. His mood swings with Sally serve a similar purpose. When he first sees her, he is convinced he is in love with her. He then alternates between annoyance and rapturous passion for the duration of their date, until he finally tells her that she gives him "a royal pain in the ass." Sally's coldness and her lack of compassion are reflective of the greater world's lack of concern about Holden's plight. Except for Jane and Phoebe, no one in his world seems to care how he feels, so long as he observes social norms. Only when his actions violate those norms does anyone notice his disturbed state, and even then, their usual response, like Sally's, is to criticize him. Despite the fact that Sally is obviously not a good match for him, Holden claims that at the moment he proposed that they run away together, he did truly love her. His feelings are irrational, but they indicate how desperate he is to find love.

This desperate need for love is counterbalanced by his inability to deal with the complexities of the real world. Like his encounter with the nuns in Chapter 15, his date with Sally demonstrates how ill-equipped he is to deal with actual people. Sally does not seem to be a very complex character, but Holden cannot connect with her at all. His wild proposals are not the kind of thing Sally is interested in, and he displays callousness when he insults her. As Holden proposes impossible schemes only to lash out when their ridiculousness is made apparent, his oversimplified, idealized fantasy world begins to seem less endearing and more dangerous.

After the fiasco with Sally, Holden retreats into nostalgic desires to return to childhood. In recalling his visits to the Museum of Natural History, Holden indicates that he wants life to be like the tableaux he loves: frozen, unchanging, simple, and readily comprehensible. He says that he wishes that everything in life could be placed inside glass cages and preserved, like in the museum. His encounter with Sally shows that he cannot deal with the complexity, conflict, and change of real life. In the museum's world, communication is unidirectional: Holden can judge the exhibits, but the exhibits cannot judge him back. After he upsets Sally, he feels terrible and tries desperately to set things right, but he fails, and he cannot tolerate the stressful situation in which he has enmeshed himself. Isolation, he finds, is simpler than the stress that accompanies conflict.

Holden's nostalgic love of the museum is rather tragic: it represents his hopeless fantasizing, his inability to deal with the real world, and his unwillingness to think about his own shortcomings. He mentions that every time he returns to the museum, he is disturbed because he has changed while the displays have not. But he is unwilling to probe further. He readily admits that he can't explain what he means, and probably wouldn't want to even if he could. Holden is unwilling to confront his own problems,

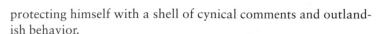

protecting himself with a shell of cynical comments and outlandish behavior.

## CHAPTERS 18–20

### SUMMARY: CHAPTER 18

After leaving the skating rink, Holden goes to a drugstore and has a Swiss cheese sandwich and a malted milk. Once again, he thinks about calling Jane, but his mind begins to wander. He remembers the time he saw her at a dance with a boy Holden thought was a show-off, but Jane argued that the boy had an inferiority complex. Holden decides that girls always say that as an excuse to date arrogant boys. Finally, he calls Jane, but no one answers. He then calls a boy named Carl Luce, whom he used to know at the Whooton School, and Luce agrees to meet him for drinks later that night.

To kill time, Holden goes to see a movie at Radio City Music Hall. He finds the Rockettes' Christmas stage show ridiculous and superficial, but it makes him remember how he and Allie used to love the kettledrum player in the Radio City pit orchestra. The man was an unnoticed, minuscule part of the show, but he seemed to take joy and pride in what he did. After the show, the movie begins, which Holden claims to find boring as well. When it is over, he begins walking to the Wicker Bar, where he is supposed to meet Luce. The movie was about the war, so Holden thinks about the army. Based on what D. B. has told him, Holden decides that he could never be in the military. He would rather, he says, be shot by a firing squad or sit on top of an atom bomb.

### SUMMARY: CHAPTER 19

At the Wicker Bar, located in the posh Seton Hotel, Holden thinks about Luce. Luce is three years older than Holden and now a student at Columbia University. At the Whooton School, Luce used to tell the younger boys about sex. Holden says that he finds Luce amusing, even though he is effeminate and a phony. When Luce arrives, he treats Holden coolly, and Holden pesters him with questions about sex. Luce refuses to be drawn into the kind of sex discussion that they had had at Whooton, and he suggests that Holden needs psychoanalysis. Holden remembers that Luce's father is a psychoanalyst, but Luce is evasive when Holden asks whether Luce's father ever analyzed his own son. Annoyed by Holden's juvenile comments and questions, Luce departs.

## Summary: Chapter 20

After Luce leaves, Holden stays at the bar and gets very drunk. He stumbles to the phone booth and makes an incoherent late-night call to Sally Hayes, angering both her and her grandmother. He then tries to make a date with the lounge singer, an attractive woman named Valencia. When that fails, he tries, with no more success, to make a date with the hat-check girl.

He decides to walk to the duck pond in Central Park to see if the ducks are still around. Along the way, he becomes quite upset when he drops and breaks the record he had bought for Phoebe. Because he had splashed water in his hair at the hotel in an attempt to sober up, his hair begins to freeze and fill with icicles. At the duck pond, he worries about catching pneumonia and imagines his funeral. He missed Allie's funeral, he says, because he was in the hospital after breaking the garage windows with his bare hands. He remembers going to Allie's grave with his parents. He becomes disgusted and sad, because the idea of placing flowers on the grass that covers the stomachs of the dead disturbs him.

Holden wants to talk to Phoebe, and he is running low on money, so he decides to risk going home. He expects his parents to be asleep, which will allow him to sneak in, speak with Phoebe, and then leave without being heard. He leaves the park and begins the long walk home.

---

## Analysis: Chapters 18–20

Holden's off-kilter ramblings in Chapter 18 about being killed by an atom bomb sound like the bravado of a frightened, threatened boy. We have seen Holden's bravado throughout the novel—when he worries that he is a coward, when he screams at Maurice, when he imagines himself as a vengeful movie character seeking justice through extreme force. But bravado is most important in this section because Holden's interaction with the effeminate Carl Luce causes him to exhibit a subtle vein of homophobia that will be important later in the novel. Like many adolescent boys, Holden is uncomfortable with sexuality and especially uncomfortable with the idea of homosexuality. Though Luce seems to prefer women, Holden finds him slightly "flitty," and Luce brings out an unpleasant lewdness in Holden's behavior.

Holden aggressively questions Luce about sex and seems to feel titillated throughout their conversation. Holden clearly wants Luce to give him some kind of guidance and insight into adult sexuality, but his attempts to raise the subject are clumsy and immature, and Luce refuses to interact with Holden on the same footing that they had at Whooton. When Luce leaves, Holden feels depressed and uncomfortable, and we get the sense that he is disappointed in himself—that despite his protestations that Luce is a phony, he wanted to connect with him and failed. With each successive interaction, Holden loses more faith in himself. He withdraws deeper into his cynicism, while at the same time feeling more and more desperate to break out of his loneliness. After Luce departs, Holden gets extremely drunk and acts completely unhinged. He hits on Valencia and the hat-check girl and then senselessly breaks into tears before walking through the freezing cold to the duck pond.

Though Holden does not acknowledge his imbalances, we again see how little control Holden has over both himself and his worsening situation. Holden's lack of introspection deepens our sense of the danger in which he finds himself. His thoughts as he walks to the pond reveal what may lie at the root of his manic behavior: he is upset and miserable at the memory of Allie's death. His memory of leaving flowers on Allie's grave leads him to another one of his defensive understatements. He was obviously shaken by the trips to the cemetery, but all he says in his narration is that he used to go with his parents, but he stopped accompanying them because he "certainly didn't enjoy seeing him in that crazy cemetery." The conjunction of Allie's memory with the image of the duck pond helps to explain Holden's preoccupation with the pond and establishes it as one of *The Catcher in the Rye*'s key symbols. Allie is gone forever, and Holden does not believe in afterlife; his atheism was mentioned in Chapter 14. Now, Holden is troubled by unexplained disappearances. He is anxious to know where the ducks have gone, since he feels extremely threatened by the idea that people and things just vanish, as Allie did. The pond itself becomes a minor metaphor for the world as Holden sees it. It is "partly frozen and partly not frozen," in a transitional state just like Holden himself and the world he inhabits.

Holden's curiosity about the ducks also demonstrates an appealingly childlike quality: his willingness (shared with his siblings) to pay attention to details that are conventionally ignored. Holden's interest in the kettledrum player at Radio City is another of these details. Holden associates adulthood with an unwillingness to explore subtle and mysterious questions, but there are many difficult questions that he himself is unwilling to explore. He never ponders what the duck pond means to him, why memories of Allie's death trouble him so much, or why he is having such difficulty dealing with the world around him.

## CHAPTERS 21–23

### SUMMARY: CHAPTER 21
Holden takes the elevator up to his family's apartment. Luckily for him, the regular elevator operator is gone, and he is able to convince the new one, who doesn't recognize him, that he wants to visit the Dicksteins, who live across the hall from the Caulfields.

Holden sneaks into his family's apartment and looks for Phoebe, but she isn't in her room. Holden tiptoes to D. B.'s room, because Phoebe likes to sleep there when D. B. is in Hollywood. He finds Phoebe sleeping peacefully, and he remarks that children, unlike adults, always look peaceful when they are asleep. As he watches Phoebe sleep, he reads through her schoolbooks. She has signed her name "Phoebe Weatherfield Caulfield," even though her middle name is Josephine. He enjoys reading the notes to friends, the curious questions, and the random imaginative jottings she has scribbled on the pages.

He finally wakes Phoebe, and she is overjoyed to see him. Bursting with energy, she talks feverishly about one thing after another: her school play (in which she plays Benedict Arnold), a movie she has just seen, a movie D. B. is working on, a boy at school who bullies her, and the fact that their parents are at a party and won't come home until later. But after her enthusiastic flurry of conversation, she realizes that Holden is home two days early and must have been kicked out of school. Over and over, she repeats that their father will "kill" him. Holden tries to justify his behavior, but she refuses to listen and covers her head with a pillow. Holden leaves the room to get some cigarettes.

### SUMMARY: CHAPTER 22
Holden returns to Phoebe's room and eventually gets her to listen. He tries to explain why he fails his classes and tells her all the things he hates about school. She responds by accusing him of hating everything. He tries to refute her claim, and she challenges him to name one thing he likes. He becomes preoccupied, thinking about the nuns he met at breakfast. He also thinks about James Castle, a boy he knew at Elkton Hills School who jumped out of a window to his death while being tormented by other boys.

He finally tells her that he likes Allie, and she reminds him angrily that Allie is dead. She asks what he wants to do with his life, and his only answer is to mention the lyric, "If a body catch a body comin' through the rye." Holden says that he imagines a gigantic field of rye on a cliff full of children playing. He wants to stand at the edge of the cliff and catch the children when they come too close to falling off—to be "the catcher in the rye." Phoebe points out that Holden has misheard the words—the actual lyric, from the Robert Burns poem, "Coming Thro' the Rye," is "If a body meet a body coming through the rye."

## SUMMARY: CHAPTER 23

Holden leaves Phoebe's room for a moment to call Mr. Antolini, an English teacher he had at Elkton Hills. Mr. Antolini is shocked that Holden has been kicked out of another school and invites Holden to stay the night at his house. Holden mentions to us that Mr. Antolini was the only teacher who approached James Castle's body after his death, the only one who demonstrated any courage or kindness in the situation. Holden goes back into Phoebe's room and asks her to dance. After a few numbers, they hear the front door open—their parents have come home from their dinner party. Holden tries to fan away his lingering cigarette smoke and jumps in the closet. His mother comes in to tuck Phoebe in, and he hides until she leaves. He then tells Phoebe goodbye, letting her know of his plan to leave New York and move out west alone. She loans him the Christmas money she'd been saving, and he leaves for Mr. Antolini's. On the way out, he gives Phoebe his red hunting hat.

## ANALYSIS: CHAPTERS 21–23

The scene in which Holden watches Phoebe sleep and reads through her notebooks is one of the most famous in the book, one of the few moments of respite Holden finds from the brutality of the outside world. As he says, adults "look lousy" when sleeping, but kids "look all right." After Phoebe wakes up, however, things become more difficult. Her insistence in Chapter 22 that Holden tell her something he likes sends his mind skittering away from the question, and he remembers the violent death of James Castle, who committed suicide in a turtleneck he borrowed from Holden. After remembering the death of this young boy, the only thing Holden can think to tell Phoebe he likes is "Allie." His mind is increasingly preoccupied with childhood and childhood death; he thinks to call Mr. Antolini when he remembers the teacher picking up James Castle's broken body in his coat. He grows increasingly emotional and unstable; Phoebe's unaffected kindness when she loans him her Christmas money causes him to break into tears.

> *And I'm standing on the edge of some crazy cliff. What I have to do, I have to catch everybody if they start to go over the cliff. . . .*

*(See* QUOTATIONS, *p. 54)*

One of the most important passages in the novel comes when Holden tells Phoebe he would like to be the catcher in the rye, saving little children from falling off the cliff. This passage elucidates the novel's metaphoric title. The rye field is a symbol of childhood—the rye is so high that the children cannot see over it, just as children are unable to see beyond the borders of their childhood. Standing on the precipice that separates the rye field of childhood from the cliff of adulthood, Holden wants to protect childhood innocence from the fall into disillusionment that necessarily accompanies adulthood. Trapped between states, with his innocence in jeopardy, Holden wants to be a "catcher in the rye," a savior of the innocence missing in the world around him, a world that has let him fall over the cliff into adulthood alone.

Holden's mistake about the line from the Robert Burns song—his substitution of "catch a body" for "meet a body"—is highly significant, as its placement in the novel's title suggests. Burns's song "Comin' Thro' the Rye" exists in several versions, each with somewhat different lyrics. In some versions, the song is about a woman who has gotten her clothes wet while she was out in a rye field, while in other versions the speaker of the song is a woman discussing being out in a rye field. All versions of the song ask the question: is it wrong to "kiss" and "greet" someone you are attracted to if you meet them out in the fields, even if you don't tell the rest of the world about it and you aren't committed to that person? Implicitly, the song asks if casual sex, in the sense of sex without a commitment, is always wrong. Thus, in Burns's song, "meeting" means encountering a potential sex partner, and the word itself may even connote having sex with that person. Casual sex is precisely the kind of sex that Holden finds most upsetting throughout the novel. By "catching" children from falling off a cliff, he really wants to protect them from the fall out of innocence into the adult world. In Chapter 25, Holden is quite explicit that he specifically wants to protect children

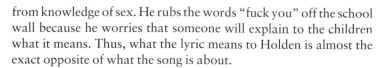

from knowledge of sex. He rubs the words "fuck you" off the school wall because he worries that someone will explain to the children what it means. Thus, what the lyric means to Holden is almost the exact opposite of what the song is about.

## CHAPTER 24

### SUMMARY

When Holden arrives at Mr. Antolini's, Mr. Antolini and his wife have just wrapped up a dinner party in their upscale Sutton Place apartment. Glasses and dishes are everywhere, and Holden can tell that Mr. Antolini has been drinking. Holden takes a seat, and the two begin talking. As Mrs. Antolini prepares coffee, Mr. Antolini inquires about Holden's expulsion from Pencey Prep. Holden reveals that he disliked the rules and regulations at Pencey Prep. As an example, he mentions his debate class in which students were penalized for digressing from their subject. Holden argues that digressions are more interesting. Instead of offering complete sympathy, Mr. Antolini gently challenges Holden, pointing out that digressions are often distracting, and that sometimes it is more interesting and appropriate to stick to the topic. Holden begins to see the weakness of his argument and becomes uncomfortable. But Mrs. Antolini cuts the tension, bringing coffee for Holden and Mr. Antolini before going to bed.

> *"I have a feeling that you're riding for some kind of terrible, terrible fall."*
>
> *(See* QUOTATIONS, *p. 55)*

After this respite, Mr. Antolini resumes the discussion on a much more serious note. He tells Holden that he is worried about him because he seems primed for a major fall, a fall that will leave him frustrated and embittered against the rest of the world, particularly against the sort of boys he hated at school. At this suggestion Holden becomes defensive and argues that he actually, after a while, grows to semi-like guys like Ackley and Stradlater. After an awkward silence, Mr. Antolini further explains the "fall" he is envisioning, saying that it is experienced by men who cannot deal with the environment around them. But he tells Holden that if he applies himself in school, he will learn that many men and women have been similarly disturbed and troubled by the human condition, and he will also learn a great deal about his own mind. Holden seems interested in what Mr. Antolini has to say, but he is exhausted. Finally, he is unable to suppress a yawn. Mr. Antolini chuckles, makes up the couch, and, after some small talk about girls, lets Holden go to sleep.

Suddenly, Holden wakes up; he feels Mr. Antolini's hand stroking his head. Mr. Antolini claims it was nothing, but Holden believes Mr. Antolini is making a homosexual advance and hurries out of the apartment.

---

## ANALYSIS

At first, Mr. Antolini seems to offer Holden his only chance of making a sympathetic connection with an adult. Holden respects his teacher's intelligence and seems legitimately interested in Mr. Antolini's lecture about finding "what size mind you have." It is significant that Holden consistently refers to his former teacher as "Mr. Antolini," whereas he refers to Mr. Spencer as "old Spencer" or "Spencer." But a subtly menacing undercurrent runs through Holden's description of his time at the Antolinis': the unwashed glasses from the dinner party, Mrs. Antolini's unattractive appearance without her makeup, and Mr. Antolini's excessive drinking all contribute to a feeling of discomfort that Holden never explicitly acknowledges. When Holden wakes to find Mr. Antolini stroking his head, he snaps. The pressure of his surging sexual feelings, combined with the nervous homophobia he exhibited around Carl Luce, make Mr. Antolini's gesture more than he can handle, and he leaves Mr. Antolini's apartment awkwardly and hastily.

The question of whether Mr. Antolini really made a homosexual advance on Holden is much more complicated than Holden implies. Holden might be right—Antolini's inquiries about Holden's girlfriends and the fact that he calls Holden "handsome" as he wishes him goodnight could be read as flirtatious advances. But it seems far more likely that Mr. Antolini's gesture was simply a tipsy sign of affection for a student in obvious pain, a student in whom Mr. Antolini sensed something fragile and genuine. But, as with everything else, Holden is rash and uncompromising in his interpretation of his teacher's behavior, and, with that rash interpretation, all of Holden's trust and faith in Mr. Antolini vanish. Mr. Antolini is clearly a more complex and multidimensional character than Holden makes him out to be. But, as we have already seen, what little stability Holden has left depends on his maintaining an oversimplified worldview— he cannot tolerate motives that are at all ambiguous. Throughout the scene, we remain as puzzled as Holden is as to what is really going on, which allows us to empathize with Holden in the crisis he experiences as a result of the encounter.

The fact that Mr. Antolini is trying to prevent Holden from "a fall" obviously parallels Holden's image of the "catcher in the rye." Yet, Mr. Antolini is a very different kind of catcher from the one Holden envisioned, and the type of fall he describes is different from the one Holden imagines. Holden fantasizes about protecting children from adulthood and sexuality (see Chapter 25), but Mr. Antolini describes the more frightening fall that will come if Holden himself refuses to grow up. Holden maintains an idealized view of childhood, and simplified view of adulthood, in order to justify his withdrawal from society. He resists intimacy because the complexities of real-world relationships collapse his simplistic perspective. Mr. Antolini's trenchant criticism forces Holden to see his own problems, while the ambiguity of his motives force him to encounter the complexity and ambiguity of the adult world. As such, he is beginning to see the trap of painful loneliness and isolation he has created for himself with his largely self-imposed alienation.

## CHAPTERS 25–26

### SUMMARY: CHAPTER 25

After leaving Mr. Antolini's, Holden goes to Grand Central Station and spends the night sleeping on a bench in the waiting room. The next day, he walks up and down Fifth Avenue, watching the children and feeling more and more nervous and overwhelmed. Every time he crosses a street, he feels like he will disappear, so each time he reaches a curb, he calls to Allie, pleading with his dead brother to let him make it to the other side. He decides to leave New York, hitchhike west, and never go home or to school again. He imagines living as a hermit, never talking to anybody, and marrying a deaf-mute girl.

He goes to Phoebe's school and writes her a note telling her to meet him at the Museum of Art so he can return the money she lent him. As he wanders around his old school, he becomes even more depressed when he finds the words "fuck you" scrawled on the walls.

While waiting at the museum, Holden shows two young kids where the mummies are. He leads them down the hallway to the tomb exhibit, but they get scared and run off, leaving Holden alone in the dark, cramped passage. Holden likes it at first, but then sees another "fuck you" written on the wall. Disgusted, he speculates that when he dies, somebody will probably write the words "fuck you" on his tombstone. He leaves the exhibit to wait for Phoebe. On the way to the bathroom, he passes out, but he downplays the incident.

Phoebe arrives at the museum with a suitcase and begs Holden to take her with him. He feels dizzy and worries that he will pass out again. He tells her that she cannot possibly go with him and feels even closer to fainting. She gets angry, refuses to look at him, and gruffly returns his hunting hat. Holden tells her he won't go away and asks her to go back to school. She angrily refuses, and he offers to take her to the zoo.

They walk to the zoo, Holden on one side of the street, Phoebe following angrily on the other. After looking at some animals, they walk to the park, now on the same side of the street, although still not quite together. They come to the carousel, and Holden convinces Phoebe to ride it. He sits on a park bench, watching her go around and around. They have reconciled, he is wearing his red hunting hat, and suddenly he feels so happy he thinks he might cry.

## SUMMARY: CHAPTER 26

Holden concludes his story by refusing to discuss what happened after his day in the park with Phoebe, although he does say that he went home, got sick, and was sent to the rest home from which he now tells his story. He says he is supposed to go to a new school in the fall and thinks that he will apply himself there, but he doesn't feel like talking about it. He wishes he hadn't talked about his experiences so much in the first place, even to D. B., who often comes to visit him in the rest home. Talking about what happened to him makes him miss all the people in his story.

---

## ANALYSIS: CHAPTERS 25–26

Holden's breakdown reaches its climax in Chapter 25. As the chapter begins, Holden feels surrounded on all sides by ugliness and phoniness—the profanity on the walls, the vulgar Christmas-tree delivery men, the empty pomp of Christmas—and his recent interactions with Phoebe and Mr. Antolini have left him feeling completely lonely and alienated. As he wanders the streets of New York, he looks at children and prays to Allie to keep him from disappearing as the ducks disappeared and as Allie himself disappeared. It's clear that Mr. Antolini was, at least in part, correct: Holden does not feel connected to his environment. He imagines that he is an ephemeral presence that will instantaneously vanish. Not only does he feel that he cannot relate to anybody, but he doesn't know how to deal with adult encounters, because they don't fit neatly into the worldview he has constructed for himself. As a result, he makes the only decision that seems logical in such a situation: he decides to run away. Unable to deal with the world around him, and realizing that his cynical view of the world is not grounded in reality, he decides to leave.

Phoebe demands to go with Holden, but it is unclear whether she needs him or whether she worries that he needs her. Despite her young age, it's safe to assume that she has a clearer perspective on the situation than Holden, so the latter explanation seems more likely. Nevertheless, Holden sees the effect his plans have on someone he cares about—a first sign of true maturity. He begins to come out of his shell, demonstrating concern for Phoebe and a willingness to love people around him. After Holden makes the decision to stay and Phoebe forgives him, she returns his hunting hat, reciprocating his gesture of kindness. It is the only moment of reciprocal interaction that Holden experiences in the book: from Stradlater to Sally Hayes, most characters just want to take things from him or use him for a specific purpose. The few characters who try to give Holden something, like Mr. Spencer or Mr. Antolini, find that Holden is unwilling to reciprocate. He remains suspicious of accepting their advice and unwilling to communicate. But here, he and Phoebe demonstrate true interaction, both selflessly giving and humbly taking from each other. It is the kind of intimacy Holden has been longing for and sorely missing.

When Holden watches Phoebe go around and around on the carousel, he finds himself deliriously happy as he participates in a scene of childhood joy and innocence. With Phoebe, he seems to have found the human contact he was looking for. The implication is that now, perhaps, he can begin the process of introspection and healing that he needs.

In Chapter 26, despite his refusal to talk any more about his story, Holden nevertheless fills in some key missing details: he went home; he was sent to a rest home to recover from the breakdown; he's in psychotherapy; and he'll go to a new school in the fall. Holden's defensively cynical tone continues throughout the chapter, which raises the question of whether the novel's ending is tragic. He says he plans to apply himself in school next year and seems contemplative, but he is unable to express his feelings and says that he wishes he hadn't told so many people his story.

The novel's ending is ambiguous. It is unclear whether Holden will fulfill the promise of recovery that is suggested as he watches the carousel. Holden's final statement—"Don't tell anybody anything. If you do, you start missing everybody"— suggests that he is still shackled by the same problems he has dealt with throughout the book. He still seems scared and alone, and he continues to dread communication. On the other hand, his final words suggest that he has begun to shed the impenetrable skin of cynicism that he had grown around himself. He has begun to value, rather than dismiss, the people around him. His nostalgia—"missing everybody"—reveals that he is not as bitter and repressed as he was earlier in the book.

# Important Quotations Explained

1. "Life is a game, boy. Life is a game that one plays according to the rules."

   "Yes, sir. I know it is. I know it."

   Game, my ass. Some game. If you get on the side where all the hot-shots are, then it's a game, all right—I'll admit that. But if you get on the other side, where there aren't any hot-shots, then what's a game about it? Nothing. No game.

This quotation is from Holden's conversation with Spencer in Chapter 2. His former teacher is needling him about his failures at Pencey; at this point, he lectures Holden about the importance of playing by the rules. The conversation succinctly illuminates key aspects of Holden's character. We see his silent contempt for adults, which is evidenced by the silent ridiculing and cursing of Spencer that Holden hides beneath his nodding, compliant veneer. We also see how alienated he feels. He clearly identifies with those on the "other side" of the game, and he feels alone and victimized, as though the world is against him. At this point in the novel, Holden's sense of disadvantage and corresponding bitterness seem somewhat strange, given his circumstances: he's clearly a bright boy from a privileged New York family. As the book progresses, however, we learn that Holden has built a cynical psychological armor around himself to protect himself from the complexities of the world.

2.    [Ackley] took another look at my hat . . . "Up home we
      wear a hat like that to shoot deer in, for Chrissake," he
      said. "That's a deer shooting hat."
          "Like hell it is." I took it off and looked at it. I sort of
      closed one eye, like I was taking aim at it. "This is a people
      shooting hat," I said. "I shoot people in this hat."

This brief passage occurs in Chapter 3, after Holden has returned
to his dorm room and is being pestered by Ackley. Of all the places
in the novel where Holden discusses his hat, the most famous and
recognizable symbol in the book, this is probably the most enlight-
ening. It is obvious from the start that Holden uses the hat as a
mark of individuality and independence. Here, we see how deeply
his desire for independence is connected to his feeling of alienation,
to the bitterness he has for the rest of the world. Of course, Holden
will not really shoot people in this hat, but it remains a symbol of his
scorn for convention. Holden nevertheless does "shoot people" in
his own way: when he is in this cynical frame of mind, he expends all
of his mental energy denigrating the people around him. He desires
independence because he feels that the world is an inhospitable,
ugly place that, he feels, deserves only contempt.

QUOTATIONS

3. The best thing, though, in that museum was that everything always stayed right where it was. Nobody'd move. . . . Nobody'd be different. The only thing that would be different would be you.

This passage, in which Holden explains why he loves the Museum of Natural History, is located in Chapter 16. Killing time before his date with Sally, Holden decides to walk from Central Park to the Museum of Natural History. Along the way, he remembers in detail his school trips to the museum. Holden has already demonstrated that he fears and does not know how to deal with conflict, confusion, and change. The museum presents him with a vision of life he can understand: it is frozen, silent, and always the same. Holden can think about and judge the Eskimo in the display case, but the Eskimo will never judge him back. It troubles him that he has changed each time he returns, while the museum's displays remain completely the same. They represent the simple, idealistic, manageable vision of life that Holden wishes he could live.

It is significant that in the final sentence Holden uses the second-person pronoun "you" instead of the first-person "me." It seems to be an attempt to distance himself from the inevitable process of change. But the impossibility of such a fantasy is the tragedy of Holden's situation: rather than face the challenges around him, he retreats to a fantasy world of his own making. When he actually gets to the museum, he decides not to go in; that would require disturbing his fragile imaginative construction by making it encounter the real world. He wants life to remain frozen like the display cases in the museum.

QUOTATIONS

4.    . . . I'm standing on the edge of some crazy cliff. What
      I have to do, I have to catch everybody if they start to
      go over the cliff—I mean if they're running and they
      don't look where they're going I have to come out from
      somewhere and catch them. That's all I'd do all day. I'd just
      be the catcher in the rye and all.

This, the passage in which Holden reveals the source of the book's
title, is perhaps the most famous in the book. It occurs in Chapter
22, after Holden has slipped quietly back into his apartment and
is speaking with Phoebe. They talk, argue, and then reconcile, and
Phoebe asks Holden what he wants to do with his life. Holden responds with this image, which reveals his fantasy of idealistic childhood and of his role as the protector of innocence. His response
makes sense, given what we already know about Holden: he prefers
to retreat into his own imaginary view of the world rather than deal
with the complexities of the world around him. He has a cynical,
oversimplified view of other people, and a large part of his fantasy
world is based on the idea that children are simple and innocent
while adults are superficial and hypocritical. The fact that he is
having this conversation with Phoebe, a child who is anything but
simple and innocent, reveals the oversimplification of his worldview. Holden himself realizes this to a degree when he acknowledges
that his idea is "crazy," yet he cannot come up with anything more
pragmatic; he has trouble seeing the world in any other way. His
catcher in the rye fantasy reflects his innocence, his belief in pure,
uncorrupted youth, and his desire to protect that spirit; on the other
hand, it represents his extreme disconnection from reality and his
naïve view of the world.

5. "I have a feeling that you're riding for some kind of terrible, terrible fall. . . . The whole arrangement's designed for men who, at some time or other in their lives, were looking for something their own environment couldn't supply them with. . . . So they gave up looking."

The conversation in which Mr. Antolini speaks these words takes place in Chapter 24. Holden has just left his parents' apartment, following his conversation with Phoebe, and he is reaching a point of critical instability, having just burst into tears when Phoebe lent him her Christmas money. He goes to Mr. Antolini's because he feels he can trust and confide in him—it seems to be his final chance to save himself. But Holden's interaction with Mr. Antolini is the event that precipitates his full-blown breakdown. It completely unsettles him, and leaves him feeling confused and unsure. While most of Holden's confusion stems from what he interprets as a homosexual come-on from Mr. Antolini, some of it stems from the conversation they have. Both the conversation and Mr. Antolini's head-rubbing serve a similar purpose: they upset Holden's view of the way things are or the way he believes they ought to be.

Mr. Antolini's words here resonate with the desires Holden has just expressed to Phoebe: like the catcher in the rye that Holden envisions, Mr. Antolini is trying to catch Holden in the midst of a "fall." But the fall Mr. Antolini describes is very different from the one Holden had imagined. Holden pictured an idyllic world of childhood innocence from which children would fall into a dangerous world; Mr. Antolini describes Holden in an apathetic free fall—giving up, disengaging himself from the world, falling in a void removed from life around him. In both cases, we sense that although Holden envisions himself as the protector rather than the one to be protected, he is the one who really needs to be caught. Mr. Antolini guesses that Holden feels disconnected from his environment, and, as we have already seen, his assessment is accurate. Holden has isolated himself in an attempt to be his own savior, but Mr. Antolini's image of falling presents a more accurate image of what awaits Holden on the other side of the "cliff." It thus reveals the weaknesses of Holden's romantic outlook.

# KEY FACTS

FULL TITLE
*The Catcher in the Rye*

AUTHOR
J. D. Salinger

TYPE OF WORK
Novel

GENRE
Bildungsroman (coming-of-age novel)

LANGUAGE
English

TIME AND PLACE WRITTEN
Late 1940s–early 1950s, New York

DATE OF FIRST PUBLICATION
July 1951; parts of the novel appeared as short stories
in *Collier's*, December 1945, and in *The New Yorker*,
December 1946

PUBLISHER
Little, Brown and Company

NARRATOR
Holden Caulfield, narrating from a psychiatric facility a few
months after the events of the novel

POINT OF VIEW
Holden Caulfield narrates in the first person, describing what
he himself sees and experiences, providing his own commentary
on the events and people he describes.

TONE
Holden's tone varies between disgust, cynicism, bitterness, and
nostalgic longing, all expressed in a colloquial style.

TENSE
Past

SETTING (TIME)

A long weekend in the late 1940s or early 1950s

SETTING (PLACE)

Holden begins his story in Pennsylvania, at his former school, Pencey Prep. He then recounts his adventures in New York City.

PROTAGONIST

Holden Caulfield

MAJOR CONFLICT

The major conflict is within Holden's psyche. Part of him wants to connect with other people on an adult level (and, more specifically, to have a sexual encounter), while part of him wants to reject the adult world as "phony," and to retreat into his own memories of childhood.

RISING ACTION

Holden's many attempts to connect with other people over the course of the novel bring his conflicting impulses—to interact with other people as an adult, or to retreat from them as a child—into direct conflict.

CLIMAX

Possible climaxes include Holden's encounter with Sunny, when it becomes clear that he is unable to handle a sexual encounter; the end of his date with Sally, when he tries to get her to run away with him; and his departure from Mr. Antolini's apartment, when he begins to question his characteristic mode of judging other people.

FALLING ACTION

Holden's interactions with Phoebe, culminating in his tears of joy at watching Phoebe on the carousel (at the novel's end he has retreated into childhood, away from the threats of adult intimacy and sexuality)

THEMES

Alienation as a form of self-protection; the painfulness of growing up; the phoniness of the adult world

MOTIFS

Relationships, intimacy, and sexuality; loneliness; lying and deception

SYMBOLS

The "catcher in the rye"; Holden's red hunting hat; the Museum of Natural History; the ducks in the Central Park lagoon

FORESHADOWING

At the beginning of the novel, Holden hints that he has been hospitalized for a nervous breakdown, the story of which is revealed over the course of the novel.

# STUDY QUESTIONS

1.  *Holden narrates the story of* THE CATCHER IN THE RYE
    *while he is recovering from his breakdown. Do you
    think the promise of recovery that Holden experiences
    as he watches the carousel at the end of the novel has
    been fulfilled? Specifically, has Holden gained a more
    mature perspective on the events that he narrates?*

It is possible that Holden is simply trying to recapture his original
emotions and thoughts in his narration, and thus masking the fact
that he has a more enlightened view regarding his behavior than
he had during his escapades. But nothing he says seems to point to
such irony on Holden's part. Although Holden narrates his story
after it has already happened, he seems to have gained little perspective. He alludes to his present situation only twice—once at the
beginning and once at the end of the novel—and he refuses to tell
us much about it. Additionally, many of the personal characteristics
that have been damaging to him—for example, his cynicism and his
lack of introspection—are in fact more pervasive in his narration of
his story than in the story itself. As a result, the story he tells is only
partial; he often glides over moments of particular trauma or treats
painful moments by pretending not to care.

    Because Holden is an unreliable narrator, in order to understand
his character it is necessary to look beyond his words at his behavior
and his interactions with others, using the knowledge of his personality acquired from his narration and applying it to his actions
in the story. For instance, when Holden tells about being beaten
and robbed by Maurice, the elevator operator, he admits that he
thought he was dying and fantasizes about being a movie hero and
seeking his revenge. But he never describes how any of this makes
him feel; his sole comment is that the "goddam movies" can ruin a
person. Since we have learned from previous moments in the book
that Holden is a deeply sensitive boy, we can look beneath the surface of his narrative to see the suffering it covers up. In this scene, we
also see how self-conflicted Holden is: he claims to hate movies, but
he turns to them in a moment of crisis. Because the relationship between the events that Holden narrates and his explanations of those

events is so complex and contradictory, and because he is unwilling to discuss any part of his "recovery," nothing that Holden says suggests that he has really matured from his experiences.

2.    *What is the significance of the carousel in Chapter 25?*

Holden's release at the end of his story comes as he watches Phoebe ride the carousel. There is an element of magic to the moment, as the carousel is operating even though it is wintertime. Holden mentions that Phoebe protests, arguing that she is too big to ride the carousel, but Holden knows that she wants to do it and he buys her a ticket. Holden, on the other hand, declines to ride, which shows him recognizing, if not accepting, his status as an adult.

In a way, the carousel is reminiscent of the statues in the Museum of Natural History, because, like them, it never changes. It continues to move in circles and always stays in the same pace; it stays the same while the children who ride it continue to grow older. It would seem, then, that the pleasure Holden takes in watching Phoebe ride is, like his moments at the museum and watching Phoebe sleep, self-deceptive.

But Holden does show some signs of growth. He comments: "All the kids kept trying to grab for the gold ring, and so was old Phoebe . . . but I didn't say anything . . . if they want to grab the gold ring, you have to let them do it . . . If they fall off, they fall off." Holden's pronouncement references his emendation of his "catcher in the rye" fantasy. Now he has come to terms with the idea that every child will eventually "fall"—out of innocence and into adulthood. Holden cannot prevent them from doing it or save them, just as he cannot prevent or save himself from becoming an adult. This recognition brings about a huge emotional release for him, and he begins to cry; the sky emulates him with a thunderstorm. Most of the other adults take refuge under the carousel's canopy, but Holden stays out in the rain. Whether we are meant to take this action as one of defiance or acceptance is, like the remainder of the novel's ending, unclear.

3.   *Though Holden never describes his psychological*
     *breakdown directly, it becomes clear as the novel*
     *progresses that he is growing increasingly unstable.*
     *How does Salinger indicate this instability to the*
     *reader while protecting his narrator's reticence?*

Salinger uses two main techniques with great efficiency. The first is
to emphasize a contrast between Holden's relatively casual description of his actions and the apparent desperation of the actions themselves. When Holden describes walking to the Central Park duck
pond late at night, for instance, he casually mentions that he had
icicles in his hair and worried about catching pneumonia, but he
does not seem to consider it strange to walk outdoors with wet hair
in freezing weather. It does seem strange to the reader, however, and
Salinger uses that sense of strangeness, as well as Holden's apparent
obliviousness to it, to emphasize his mental imbalance. His other
technique is to provide alternative viewpoints in the other characters' responses to Holden's behavior as guidelines. For instance,
when Holden has his meltdown with Sally and tries to persuade
her to flee society and live with him in a cabin, she repeatedly asks
him to stop shouting. In his account of the scene, Holden claims he
wasn't shouting, but we believe Sally. Salinger uses her angry, fearful
response to signal to the reader that Holden's mental state is worse
than he admits or acknowledges.

# How to Write
## Literary Analysis

## The Literary Essay: A Step-by-Step Guide

When you read for pleasure, your only goal is enjoyment. You might find yourself reading to get caught up in an exciting story, to learn about an interesting time or place, or just to pass time. Maybe you're looking for inspiration, guidance, or a reflection of your own life. There are as many different, valid ways of reading a book as there are books in the world.

When you read a work of literature in an English class, however, you're being asked to read in a special way: you're being asked to perform *literary analysis*. To analyze something means to break it down into smaller parts and then examine how those parts work, both individually and together. Literary analysis involves examining all the parts of a novel, play, short story, or poem—elements such as character, setting, tone, and imagery—and thinking about how the author uses those elements to create certain effects.

A literary essay isn't a book review: you're not being asked whether or not you liked a book or whether you'd recommend it to another reader. A literary essay also isn't like the kind of book report you wrote when you were younger, where your teacher wanted you to summarize the book's action. A high school- or college-level literary essay asks, "How does this piece of literature actually work?" "How does it do what it does?" and, "Why might the author have made the choices he or she did?"

### The Seven Steps
No one is born knowing how to analyze literature; it's a skill you learn and a process you can master. As you gain more practice with this kind of thinking and writing, you'll be able to craft a method that works best for you. But until then, here are seven basic steps to writing a well-constructed literary essay:

1. *Ask questions*
2. *Collect evidence*
3. *Construct a thesis*

*4. Develop and organize arguments*
*5. Write the introduction*
*6. Write the body paragraphs*
*7. Write the conclusion*

---

### 1. ASK QUESTIONS

When you're assigned a literary essay in class, your teacher will often provide you with a list of writing prompts. Lucky you! Now all you have to do is choose one. Do yourself a favor and pick a topic that interests you. You'll have a much better (not to mention easier) time if you start off with something you enjoy thinking about. If you are asked to come up with a topic by yourself, though, you might start to feel a little panicked. Maybe you have too many ideas—or none at all. Don't worry. Take a deep breath and start by asking yourself these questions:

- **What struck you?** Did a particular image, line, or scene linger in your mind for a long time? If it fascinated you, chances are you can draw on it to write a fascinating essay.

- **What confused you?** Maybe you were surprised to see a character act in a certain way, or maybe you didn't understand why the book ended the way it did. Confusing moments in a work of literature are like a loose thread in a sweater: if you pull on it, you can unravel the entire thing. Ask yourself why the author chose to write about that character or scene the way he or she did and you might tap into some important insights about the work as a whole.

- **Did you notice any patterns?** Is there a phrase that the main character uses constantly or an image that repeats throughout the book? If you can figure out how that pattern weaves through the work and what the significance of that pattern is, you've almost got your entire essay mapped out.

- **Did you notice any contradictions or ironies?** Great works of literature are complex; great literary essays recognize and explain those complexities. Maybe the title (*Happy Days*) totally disagrees with the book's subject matter (hungry orphans dying in the woods). Maybe the main character acts one way around his family and a completely different way around his friends and associates. If you can find a way to explain a work's contradictory elements, you've got the seeds of a great essay.

At this point, you don't need to know exactly what you're going to say about your topic; you just need a place to begin your exploration. You can help direct your reading and brainstorming by formulating your topic as a *question,* which you'll then try to answer in your essay. The best questions invite critical debates and discussions, not just a rehashing of the summary. Remember, you're looking for something you can *prove or argue* based on evidence you find in the text. Finally, remember to keep the scope of your question in mind: is this a topic you can adequately address within the word or page limit you've been given? Conversely, is this a topic big enough to fill the required length?

## GOOD QUESTIONS
*"Are Romeo and Juliet's parents responsible for the deaths of their children?"*
*"Why do pigs keep showing up in* LORD OF THE FLIES?*"*
*"Are Dr. Frankenstein and his monster alike? How?"*

## BAD QUESTIONS
*"What happens to Scout in* TO KILL A MOCKINGBIRD?*"*
*"What do the other characters in* JULIUS CAESAR *think about Caesar?"*
*"How does Hester Prynne in* THE SCARLET LETTER *remind me of my sister?"*

---

## 2. COLLECT EVIDENCE
Once you know what question you want to answer, it's time to scour the book for things that will help you answer the question. Don't worry if you don't know what you want to say yet—right now you're just collecting ideas and material and letting it all percolate. Keep track of passages, symbols, images, or scenes that deal with your topic. Eventually, you'll start making connections between these examples and your thesis will emerge.

Here's a brief summary of the various parts that compose each and every work of literature. These are the elements that you will analyze in your essay, and which you will offer as evidence to support your arguments. For more on the parts of literary works, see the Glossary of Literary Terms at the end of this section.

LITERARY ANALYSIS

ELEMENTS OF STORY    These are the *what*s of the work—what happens, where it happens, and to whom it happens.

- **Plot:**  All of the events and actions of the work.

- **Character:**  The people who act and are acted upon in a literary work. The main character of a work is known as the *protagonist*.

- **Conflict:**  The central tension in the work. In most cases, the protagonist wants something, while opposing forces (antagonists) hinder the protagonist's progress.

- **Setting:**  When and where the work takes place. Elements of setting include location, time period, time of day, weather, social atmosphere, and economic conditions.

- **Narrator:**  The person telling the story. The narrator may straightforwardly report what happens, convey the subjective opinions and perceptions of one or more characters, or provide commentary and opinion in his or her own voice.

- **Themes:**  The main idea or message of the work—usually an abstract idea about people, society, or life in general. A work may have many themes, which may be in tension with one another.

ELEMENTS OF STYLE    These are the *how*s—how the characters speak, how the story is constructed, and how language is used throughout the work.

- **Structure and organization:**  How the parts of the work are assembled. Some novels are narrated in a linear, chronological fashion, while others skip around in time. Some plays follow a traditional three- or five-act structure, while others are a series of loosely connected scenes. Some authors deliberately leave gaps in their works, leaving readers to puzzle out the missing information. A work's structure and organization can tell you a lot about the kind of message it wants to convey.

- **Point of view:**  The perspective from which a story is told. In *first-person point of view*, the narrator involves him or herself in the story. ("I went to the store"; "We watched in horror as the bird slammed into the window.") A first-person narrator is usually the protagonist of the work, but not always. In *third-person point of view*, the narrator does not participate in the story. A third-person narrator may closely follow a specific character, recounting that individual character's thoughts or experiences, or it may be what we call an *omniscient* narrator. Omniscient narrators see and know all: they can witness any event in any time or place and are privy to the inner thoughts and feelings of all characters. Remember that the narrator and the author are not the same thing!

- **Diction:** Word choice. Whether a character uses dry, clinical language or flowery prose with lots of exclamation points can tell you a lot about his or her attitude and personality.

- **Syntax:** Word order and sentence construction. Syntax is a crucial part of establishing an author's narrative voice. Ernest Hemingway, for example, is known for writing in very short, straightforward sentences, while James Joyce characteristically wrote in long, incredibly complicated lines.

- **Tone:** The mood or feeling of the text. Diction and syntax often contribute to the tone of a work. A novel written in short, clipped sentences that use small, simple words might feel brusque, cold, or matter-of-fact.

- **Imagery:** Language that appeals to the senses, representing things that can be seen, smelled, heard, tasted, or touched.

- **Figurative language:** Language that is not meant to be interpreted literally. The most common types of figurative language are *metaphors* and *similes,* which compare two unlike things in order to suggest a similarity between them— for example, "All the world's a stage," or "The moon is like a ball of green cheese." (Metaphors say one thing *is* another thing; similes claim that one thing is *like* another thing.)

---

3. Construct a Thesis

When you've examined all the evidence you've collected and know how you want to answer the question, it's time to write your thesis statement. A *thesis* is a claim about a work of literature that needs to be supported by evidence and arguments. The thesis statement is the heart of the literary essay, and the bulk of your paper will be spent trying to prove this claim. A good thesis will be:

- **Arguable.** "*The Great Gatsby* describes New York society in the 1920s" isn't a thesis—it's a fact.

- **Provable through textual evidence**. "*Hamlet* is a confusing but ultimately very well-written play" is a weak thesis because it offers the writer's personal opinion about the book. Yes, it's arguable, but it's not a claim that can be proved or supported with examples taken from the play itself.

- **Surprising**. "Both George and Lenny change a great deal in *Of Mice and Men*" is a weak thesis because it's obvious. A really strong thesis will argue for a reading of the text that is not immediately apparent.

- **Specific.** "Dr. Frankenstein's monster tells us a lot about the human condition" is *almost* a really great thesis statement, but it's still too vague. What does the writer mean by "a lot"? *How* does the monster tell us so much about the human condition?

## GOOD THESIS STATEMENTS

**Question:** In *Romeo and Juliet*, which is more powerful in shaping the lovers' story: fate or foolishness?

**Thesis:** "Though Shakespeare defines Romeo and Juliet as 'star-crossed lovers' and images of stars and planets appear throughout the play, a closer examination of that celestial imagery reveals that the stars are merely witnesses to the characters' foolish activities and not the causes themselves."

**Question:** How does the bell jar function as a symbol in Sylvia Plath's *The Bell Jar*?

**Thesis:** "A bell jar is a bell-shaped glass that has three basic uses: to hold a specimen for observation, to contain gases, and to maintain a vacuum. The bell jar appears in each of these capacities in *The Bell Jar,* Plath's semi-autobiographical novel, and each appearance marks a different stage in Esther's mental breakdown."

**Question:** Would Piggy in *The Lord of the Flies* make a good island leader if he were given the chance?

**Thesis:** "Though the intelligent, rational, and innovative Piggy has the mental characteristics of a good leader, he ultimately lacks the social skills necessary to be an effective one. Golding emphasizes this point by giving Piggy a foil in the charismatic Jack, whose magnetic personality allows him to capture and wield power effectively, if not always wisely."

## 4. DEVELOP AND ORGANIZE ARGUMENTS

The reasons and examples that support your thesis will form the middle paragraphs of your essay. Since you can't really write your thesis statement until you know how you'll structure your argument, you'll probably end up working on steps 3 and 4 at the same time.

There's no single method of argumentation that will work in every context. One essay prompt might ask you to compare and contrast two characters, while another asks you to trace an image through a given work of literature. These questions require different kinds of answers and therefore different kinds of arguments. Below, we'll discuss three common kinds of essay prompts and some strategies for constructing a solid, well-argued case.

### TYPES OF LITERARY ESSAYS

- **Compare and contrast**

  *Compare and contrast the characters of Huck and Jim in* THE ADVENTURES OF HUCKLEBERRY FINN.

  Chances are you've written this kind of essay before. In an academic literary context, you'll organize your arguments the same way you would in any other class. You can either go *subject by subject* or *point by point*. In the former, you'll discuss one character first and then the second. In the latter, you'll choose several traits (attitude toward life, social status, images and metaphors associated with the character) and devote a paragraph to each. You may want to use a mix of these two approaches—for example, you may want to spend a paragraph a piece broadly sketching Huck's and Jim's personalities before transitioning into a paragraph or two that describes a few key points of comparison. This can be a highly effective strategy if you want to make a counterintuitive argument—that, despite seeming to be totally different, the two objects being compared are actually similar in a very important way (or vice versa). Remember that your essay should reveal something fresh or unexpected about the text, so think beyond the obvious parallels and differences.

- **Trace**

  *Choose an image—for example, birds, knives, or eyes—and trace that image throughout* MACBETH.

  Sounds pretty easy, right? All you need to do is read the play, underline every appearance of a knife in *Macbeth*, and then list them in your essay in the order they appear, right? Well, not exactly. Your teacher doesn't want a simple catalog of examples. He or she wants to see you make *connections* between those examples—that's the difference between summarizing and analyzing. In the *Macbeth* example above, think about the different contexts in which knives appear in the play and to what effect. In *Macbeth*, there are real knives and imagined knives; knives that kill and knives that simply threaten. Categorize and classify your examples to give them some order. Finally, always keep the overall effect in mind. After you choose and analyze your examples, you should come to some greater understanding about the work, as well as your chosen image, symbol, or phrase's role in developing the major themes and stylistic strategies of that work.

- **Debate**

    *Is the society depicted in* 1984 *good for its citizens?*

    In this kind of essay, you're being asked to debate a moral, ethical, or aesthetic issue regarding the work. You might be asked to judge a character or group of characters (*Is Caesar responsible for his own demise?*) or the work itself (*Is* JANE EYRE *a feminist novel?*). For this kind of essay, there are two important points to keep in mind. First, don't simply base your arguments on your personal feelings and reactions. Every literary essay expects you to read and analyze the work, so search for evidence in the text. What do characters in *1984* have to say about the government of Oceania? What images does Orwell use that might give you a hint about his attitude toward the government? As in any debate, you also need to make sure that you define all the necessary terms before you begin to argue your case. What does it mean to be a "good" society? What makes a novel "feminist"? You should define your terms right up front, in the first paragraph after your introduction.

    Second, remember that strong literary essays make contrary and surprising arguments. Try to think outside the box. In the *1984* example above, it seems like the obvious answer would be no, the totalitarian society depicted in Orwell's novel is *not* good for its citizens. But can you think of any arguments for the opposite side? Even if your final assertion is that the novel depicts a cruel, repressive, and therefore harmful society, acknowledging and responding to the counterargument will strengthen your overall case.

## 5. WRITE THE INTRODUCTION

Your introduction sets up the entire essay. It's where you present your topic and articulate the particular issues and questions you'll be addressing. It's also where you, as the writer, introduce yourself to your readers. A persuasive literary essay immediately establishes its writer as a knowledgeable, authoritative figure.

An introduction can vary in length depending on the overall length of the essay, but in a traditional five-paragraph essay it should be no longer than one paragraph. However long it is, your introduction needs to:

- **Provide any necessary context.** Your introduction should situate the reader and let him or her know what to expect. What book are you discussing? Which characters? What topic will you be addressing?

- **Answer the "So what?" question.** Why is this topic important, and why is your particular position on the topic noteworthy? Ideally, your introduction should pique the reader's interest by suggesting how your argument is surprising or otherwise counterintuitive. Literary essays make unexpected connections and reveal less-than-obvious truths.

- **Present your thesis.** This usually happens at or very near the end of your introduction.

- **Indicate the shape of the essay to come.** Your reader should finish reading your introduction with a good sense of the scope of your essay as well as the path you'll take toward proving your thesis. You don't need to spell out every step, but you do need to suggest the organizational pattern you'll be using.

Your introduction should not:

- **Be vague.** Beware of the two killer words in literary analysis: *interesting* and *important*. Of course the work, question, or example is interesting and important—that's why you're writing about it!

- **Open with any grandiose assertions.** Many student readers think that beginning their essays with a flamboyant statement such as, "Since the dawn of time, writers have been fascinated with the topic of free will," makes them sound important and commanding. You know what? It actually sounds pretty amateurish.

- **Wildly praise the work.** Another typical mistake student writers make is extolling the work or author. Your teacher doesn't need to be told that "Shakespeare is perhaps the greatest writer in the English language." You can mention a work's reputation in passing—by referring to *The Adventures of Huckleberry Finn* as "Mark Twain's enduring classic," for example—but don't make a point of bringing it up unless that reputation is key to your argument.

- **Go off-topic.** Keep your introduction streamlined and to the point. Don't feel the need to throw in all kinds of bells and whistles in order to impress your reader—just get to the point as quickly as you can, without skimping on any of the required steps.

---

### 6. WRITE THE BODY PARAGRAPHS

Once you've written your introduction, you'll take the arguments you developed in step 4 and turn them into your body paragraphs. The organization of this middle section of your essay will largely be determined by the argumentative strategy you use, but no matter how you arrange your thoughts, your body paragraphs need to do the following:

- **Begin with a strong topic sentence.** Topic sentences are like signs on a highway: they tell the reader where they are and where they're going. A good topic sentence not only alerts readers to what issue will be discussed in the following paragraph but also gives them a sense of what argument will be made *about* that issue. "Rumor and gossip play an important role in *The Crucible*" isn't a strong topic sentence because it doesn't tell us very much. "The community's constant gossiping creates an environment that allows false accusations to flourish" is a much stronger topic sentence— it not only tells us *what* the paragraph will discuss (gossip) but *how* the paragraph will discuss the topic (by showing how gossip creates a set of conditions that leads to the play's climactic action).

- **Fully and completely develop a single thought.** Don't skip around in your paragraph or try to stuff in too much material. Body paragraphs are like bricks: each individual one needs to be strong and sturdy or the entire structure will collapse. Make sure you have really proven your point before moving on to the next one.

- **Use transitions effectively.** Good literary essay writers know that each paragraph must be clearly and strongly linked to the material around it. Think of each paragraph as a response to the one that precedes it. Use transition words and phrases such as *however, similarly, on the contrary, therefore,* and *furthermore* to indicate what kind of response you're making.

---

7. WRITE THE CONCLUSION

Just as you used the introduction to ground your readers in the topic before providing your thesis, you'll use the conclusion to quickly summarize the specifics learned thus far and then hint at the broader implications of your topic. A good conclusion will:

- **Do more than simply restate the thesis.** If your thesis argued that *The Catcher in the Rye* can be read as a Christian allegory, don't simply end your essay by saying, "And that is why *The Catcher in the Rye* can be read as a Christian allegory." If you've constructed your arguments well, this kind of statement will just be redundant.

- **Synthesize the arguments, not summarize them.** Similarly, don't repeat the details of your body paragraphs in your conclusion. The reader has already read your essay, and chances are it's not so long that they've forgotten all your points by now.

- **Revisit the "So what?" question.** In your introduction, you made a case for why your topic and position are important. You should close your essay with the same sort of gesture. What do your readers know now that they didn't know before? How will that knowledge help them better appreciate or understand the work overall?

- **Move from the specific to the general.** Your essay has most likely treated a very specific element of the work—a single character, a small set of images, or a particular passage. In your conclusion, try to show how this narrow discussion has wider implications for the work overall. If your essay on *To Kill a Mockingbird* focused on the character of Boo Radley, for example, you might want to include a bit in your conclusion about how he fits into the novel's larger message about childhood, innocence, or family life.

- **Stay relevant.** Your conclusion should suggest new directions of thought, but it shouldn't be treated as an opportunity to pad your essay with all the extra, interesting ideas you came up with during your brainstorming sessions but couldn't fit into the essay proper. Don't attempt to stuff in unrelated queries or too many abstract thoughts.

- **Avoid making overblown closing statements.** A conclusion should open up your highly specific, focused discussion, but it should do so without drawing a sweeping lesson about life or human nature. Making such observations may be part of the point of reading, but it's almost always a mistake in essays, where these observations tend to sound overly dramatic or simply silly.

---

A+ Essay Checklist

Congratulations! If you've followed all the steps we've outlined above, you should have a solid literary essay to show for all your efforts. What if you've got your sights set on an A+? To write the kind of superlative essay that will be rewarded with a perfect grade, keep the following rubric in mind. These are the qualities that teachers expect to see in a truly A+ essay. How does yours stack up?

- ✓ Demonstrates a thorough understanding of the book
- ✓ Presents an original, compelling argument
- ✓ Thoughtfully analyzes the text's formal elements
- ✓ Uses appropriate and insightful examples
- ✓ Structures ideas in a logical and progressive order
- ✓ Demonstrates a mastery of sentence construction, transitions, grammar, spelling, and word choice

## Suggested Essay Topics

1. *Think about Holden's vision of the nature of childhood and adulthood. Are the two realms as separate as Holden believes them to be? Where does he fit in?*

2. *The novel is structured around Holden's encounters and interactions with other people. Does any pattern seem to emerge, or does anything change in his interactions as the novel progresses? How do Holden's encounters with adults, children, women, and his peers evolve as the novel progresses?*

3. *Throughout the book, Holden longs for intimacy with other human beings. Discuss the different types of relationships Holden attempts and the different types of intimacy in the book. What is the role of sexuality in* THE CATCHER IN THE RYE? *How do Holden's sexual relationships differ from his nonsexual encounters?*

4. *Holden often behaves like a prophet or a saint, pointing out the phoniness and wickedness in the world around him. Is Holden as perfect as he wants to be? Are there instances where he is phony and full of hypocrisy? What do these moments reveal about his character and his psychological problems?*

# A+ Student Essay

What is the significance of Mr. Antolini's actions in
Chapter 24? Was he making a pass at Holden?

Holden Caulfield's interpretation of his teacher's behavior is neither
surprising nor unwarranted. After all, the drunken Mr. Antolini
calls Holden "handsome," creeps into the room where Holden is
sleeping, and strokes the boy's hair while he sleeps. Many readers
might leap to conclude, as Holden does, that Mr. Antolini is making
a pass at his student. However, Holden himself provides clues that
suggest that Mr. Antolini's interest in him is not sexual. Rather, Mr.
Antolini sees himself as a guardian of wayward boys, the kind of
"catcher in the rye" that Holden aspires to be.

James Castle, the Elkton student who committed suicide before
the novel begins, seems to have given Mr. Antolini a burning need to
help struggling boys. Mr. Antolini's failure to see James's depression
or to save the boy after he jumped from the window permanently
changes him. Holden's initial description of his teacher's response
to Castle's death comprises just one brief paragraph, which suggests that Holden does not understand the transformative effect
James's death had on Mr. Antolini. But Salinger means for us to look
beneath the surface of Holden's quick description and see the horror
and power of the situation: the impressionable youth of the teacher
whom Holden describes as "a pretty young guy, not much older
than my brother D.B."; the bravery of touching the corpse when
no one else could bring himself to do it; the selflessness of draping a
coat over the bloody body—all of the details that Holden provides
suggest that Mr. Antolini responded to James's suicide with true
empathy, and that the incident had a profound effect on the kind
young teacher.

Mr. Antolini's lengthy exchange with Holden underlines his urge
to help young people he perceives as needy, depressed, or heading
for a fall. It is true that Mr. Antolini inquires about Holden's love
life, flatters him, and teases him. But this conversation is the same
kind of idle chitchat Mr. Antolini engages in with everyone in his
life. A witty man by nature, Mr. Antolini reflexively turns on the
charm no matter whom he's speaking to, whether it's his students or
his wife. He reserves his true passion and forcefulness for his long
speech to Holden, in which he cautions him not to die "for some

highly unworthy cause," urges him to find direction, and advises him to seek comfort and a creative outlet in education. This speech, which Holden quotes in its entirety, comprises several pages. By devoting so much space to the speech, Salinger makes it clear that Mr. Antolini's words are the most important part of this chapter. Holden also largely refrains from his usual editorializing here. By presenting Mr. Antolini's words directly, rather than filtering them through Holden, Salinger encourages the reader to make up his or her own mind about Mr. Antolini's intentions. When Holden offers his interpretation of events, it remains just that—an interpretation. The reader is not required to believe Holden's version in this case. In fact, because *The Catcher in the Rye* is usually so concerned with Holden's subjective response to the world around him, the fact that we are presented with an unvarnished account of Mr. Atonolini's speech actually casts even stronger doubt on Holden's interpretation of this particular incident.

Mr. Antolini does not see Holden as an object of lust. Rather, he sees him as a potential second James Castle. He wants to save Holden from despair just as Holden himself wants to save innocent children from the cruel truths of life. Although Holden's initial reaction to Mr. Antolini's kindness is repulsion, that does not mean that the teacher has failed. Perhaps the knowledge that there is one loving, intelligent adult in his life—a fact that Holden seems to grasp almost as soon as he leaves his teacher's apartment—is what ultimately helps save the depressed boy.

# GLOSSARY OF LITERARY TERMS

ANTAGONIST
> The entity that acts to frustrate the goals of the *protagonist*. The antagonist is usually another *character* but may also be a non-human force.

ANTIHERO / ANTIHEROINE
> A *protagonist* who is not admirable or who challenges notions of what should be considered admirable.

CHARACTER
> A person, animal, or any other thing with a personality that appears in a *narrative*.

CLIMAX
> The moment of greatest intensity in a text or the major turning point in the *plot*.

CONFLICT
> The central struggle that moves the *plot* forward. The conflict can be the *protagonist*'s struggle against fate, nature, society, or another person.

FIRST-PERSON POINT OF VIEW
> A literary style in which the *narrator* tells the story from his or her own *point of view* and refers to himself or herself as "I." The narrator may be an active participant in the story or just an observer.

HERO / HEROINE
> The principal *character* in a literary work or *narrative*.

IMAGERY
> Language that brings to mind sense-impressions, representing things that can be seen, smelled, heard, tasted, or touched.

MOTIF
> A recurring idea, structure, contrast, or device that develops or informs the major *themes* of a work of literature.

NARRATIVE
> A story.

NARRATOR
> The person (sometimes a *character*) who tells a story; the *voice* assumed by the writer. The narrator and the author of the work of literature are not the same person.

PLOT
> The arrangement of the events in a story, including the sequence in which they are told, the relative emphasis they are given, and the causal connections between events.

POINT OF VIEW
> The *perspective* that a *narrative* takes toward the events it describes.

PROTAGONIST
> The main *character* around whom the story revolves.

SETTING
> The location of a *narrative* in time and space. Setting creates mood or atmosphere.

SUBPLOT
> A secondary *plot* that is of less importance to the overall story but may serve as a point of contrast or comparison to the main plot.

SYMBOL
> An object, *character,* figure, or color that is used to represent an abstract idea or concept. Unlike an *emblem,* a symbol may have different meanings in different contexts.

SYNTAX
> The way the words in a piece of writing are put together to form lines, phrases, or clauses; the basic structure of a piece of writing.

THEME
> A fundamental and universal idea explored in a literary work.

TONE
> The author's attitude toward the subject or *characters* of a story or poem or toward the reader.

VOICE
> An author's individual way of using language to reflect his or her own personality and attitudes. An author communicates voice through *tone, diction,* and *syntax.*

LITERARY ANALYSIS

# A Note on Plagiarism

Plagiarism—presenting someone else's work as your own—rears its ugly head in many forms. Many students know that copying text without citing it is unacceptable. But some don't realize that even if you're not quoting directly, but instead are paraphrasing or summarizing, *it is plagiarism* unless you cite the source.

Here are the most common forms of plagiarism:

- Using an author's phrases, sentences, or paragraphs without citing the source
- Paraphrasing an author's ideas without citing the source
- Passing off another student's work as your own

How do you steer clear of plagiarism? You should *always* acknowledge all words and ideas that aren't your own by using quotation marks around verbatim text or citations like footnotes and endnotes to note another writer's ideas. For more information on how to give credit when credit is due, ask your teacher for guidance or visit www.sparknotes.com.

# Review & Resources

## Quiz

1. When the novel begins, Holden is

   A. Watching a football game
   B. Taking a train to New York
   C. Recuperating in some sort of psychiatric institution
   D. Riding a carousel in Central Park

2. What is the name of the school Holden is attending at the beginning of his story?

   A. The Whooton School
   B. Pencey Prep
   C. Don Bosco High
   D. Elkton Hills

3. Holden was forced to return early to school from New York because

   A. His parents caught him in their apartment.
   B. He lost the fencing team's equipment.
   C. He desperately wanted to see the final football game.
   D. He needed to see Mr. Spencer.

4. What item of clothing did Holden buy during the team's trip to New York?

   A. A hound's-tooth jacket
   B. A red hunting hat
   C. A brown derby
   D. A pink leisure suit

5. Contrasting him with the annoying and sloppy Ackley, Holden describes Stradlater as a(n)

   A. "Anal-retentive neat-freak"
   B. "Guy whose mess you don't mind"
   C. "Clean and nice roommate"
   D. "Secret slob"

6. Holden tries to punch Stradlater immediately after

   A. Stradlater refuses to answer Holden's questions about his date.
   B. Stradlater suddenly attacks him.
   C. Stradlater brags about his sexual conquests.
   D. Stradlater rips his hound's-tooth jacket.

7. Holden nostalgically remembers the way Jane Gallagher used to

   A. Talk about the Museum of Natural History
   B. Play checkers
   C. Write stories
   D. Ride her bike

8. Once back in New York, the first person Holden tries to invite for a drink is

   A. A cab driver
   B. Faith Cavendish
   C. Carl Luce
   D. Sally Hayes

9. Holden wonders about the fate of which animals in Central Park?

   A. The squirrels in the Sheep Meadow
   B. The goats in the Children's Zoo
   C. The feral dogs roaming the Nature Preserve
   D. The ducks in the lagoon

10. After Holden checks into his room at the Edmont Hotel, what does he see out of his window?

    A. A parade
    B. A flock of ducks flying away from the Central Park lagoon
    C. A variety of bizarre sex acts going on in other rooms of the hotel
    D. Jane Gallagher fooling around with Stradlater

11. According to Holden, he knew he was happy when he was

    A. Holding hands with Jane
    B. Writing essays for Mr. Spencer
    C. Fooling "phonies" with elaborate lies
    D. Listening to Ernie play piano

12. The elevator operator at the Edmont offers to get Holden

    A. Drugs
    B. Complimentary breakfast
    C. A prostitute
    D. Movie tickets

13. Holden claims he can't sleep with Sunny because

    A. He's a virgin.
    B. He loves her too much.
    C. He's mourning the death of his mother.
    D. He's just had an operation on his "clavichord."

14. After Maurice hits Holden in the crotch, what does Holden do?

    A. He repeatedly insults Maurice, resulting in further physical punishment.
    B. He punches Maurice in the face.
    C. He collapses to the floor, cursing at Sunny.
    D. He hops around the room, spewing profanities while smoke comes out of his ears.

15. After his encounter with Maurice, Holden

    A. Calls the police
    B. Calls Jane Gallagher
    C. Pretends he's a movie character who has been shot
    D. Realizes he's in love with Sunny

16. At breakfast, Holden is surprised that the nun

    A. Eats fatty foods
    B. Likes *Romeo and Juliet*
    C. Shows no remorse over stealing the collection money
    D. Spits water on her partner's face

17. What does Holden buy for Phoebe?

   A. A book titled *Out of Africa*
   B. An autographed photograph of Robert Donat
   C. A record titled "Little Shirley Beans"
   D. A pair of yellow shoes

18. According to Holden, what is "the best thing" about the Museum of Natural History?

   A. "That everything always stayed right where it was"
   B. "That no goddam phonies ever went there"
   C. "That this one crazy Indian always reminds [him] of Allie"
   D. "That the birds look exactly like the ducks in the lagoon"

19. As Holden predicted, Sally is excited to

   A. Talk about their futures
   B. Openly discuss their problems and emotions
   C. See the Lunts
   D. Listen to "Little Shirley Beans"

20. Although Phoebe's real middle name is "Josephine," she signs her name as

   A. Phoebe Weatherfield Caulfield
   B. Phoebe Allie Caulfield
   C. Phoebe Benedict Arnold Caulfield
   D. Phoebe "Mad Dog" Caulfield

21. Phoebe chastises Holden because, in her mind, he

   A. Smokes too many cigarettes
   B. Dates terrible women
   C. Is too nice
   D. Doesn't like anything

22. What or who is the "catcher in the rye"?

    A. Holden's dream job
    B. Phoebe's favorite stuffed animal
    C. An old college buddy of Holden's father
    D. A symbolically important drinking glass

23. Just before he leaves her room, Phoebe gives Holden

    A. A stern scolding
    B. A record she had bought for him
    C. Her Christmas money
    D. His red hunting hat

24. Holden leaves Mr. Antolini's apartment because

    A. Mr. Antolini passes out drunk.
    B. He feels sick.
    C. He thinks Mr. Antolini made a pass at him.
    D. Mr. Antolini throws him out.

25. As he prepares to leave New York City, Holden repeatedly
    encounters

    A. Mr. Antolini
    B. Vulgarity scrawled on walls
    C. His brother's ghost
    D. Ackley and Stradlater

# SUGGESTIONS FOR FURTHER READING

ALEXANDER, PAUL. *Salinger, a Biography.* Los Angeles: Renaissance Books, 2000.

BLOOM, HAROLD, ed. *Holden Caulfield: Bloom's Major Literary Characters.* New York: Chelsea House Publishers, 2005.

———. *J. D. Salinger.* New York: Chelsea House, 1987.

———. *J. D. Salinger's* THE CATCHER IN THE RYE. New York: Chelsea House, 1996.

CRAWFORD, CATHERINE. *If You Really Want to Hear About It: Writers on J. D. Salinger and His Work.* New York: Thunder's Mouth Press, 2006.

ENGEL, STEVEN, ed. *Readings on* THE CATCHER IN THE RYE. San Diego: Greenhaven Press, 1998.

GRUNWALD, HENRY A., ed. *Salinger: A Critical and Personal Portrait.* New York: Harper, 1962.

HAMILTON, IAN. *In Search of J. D. Salinger.* New York: Random House, 1988.

KUBICA, CHRIS and WILL HOCHMAN, eds. *Letters to J. D. Salinger.* Madison, WI: University of Wisconsin Press, 2002.

MALCOLM, JANET. "Justice for J. D. Salinger." *The New York Review of Books* (21 June 2001): 16–22.

SALZMAN, JACK. *New Essays on* THE CATCHER IN THE RYE. New York: Cambridge University Press, 1992.

# SparkNotes Literature Guides

1984
The Adventures of
   Huckleberry Finn
The Adventures of
   Tom Sawyer
The Aeneid
All Quiet on the
   Western Front
And Then There Were
   None
Angela's Ashes
Animal Farm
Anna Karenina
Anne of Green Gables
Anthem
As I Lay Dying
The Awakening
The Bean Trees
Beloved
Beowulf
Billy Budd
Black Boy
Bless Me, Ultima
The Bluest Eye
Brave New World
The Brothers
   Karamazov
The Call of the Wild
Candide
The Canterbury Tales
Catch-22
The Catcher in the Rye
The Chocolate War
The Chosen
Cold Sassy Tree
The Color Purple
The Count of Monte
   Cristo
Crime and Punishment
The Crucible
Cry, the Beloved
   Country
Cyrano de Bergerac
David Copperfield
Death of a Salesman
Death of Socrates
Diary of a Young Girl

A Doll's House
Don Quixote
Dr. Faustus
Dr. Jekyll and Mr. Hyde
Dracula
Edith Hamilton's
   Mythology
Emma
Ethan Frome
Fahrenheit 451
A Farewell to Arms
The Fellowship of the
   Rings
Flowers for Algernon
For Whom the Bell
   Tolls
The Fountainhead
Frankenstein
The Giver
The Glass Menagerie
The Good Earth
The Grapes of Wrath
Great Expectations
The Great Gatsby
Grendel
Gulliver's Travels
Hamlet
The Handmaid's Tale
Hard Times
Heart of Darkness
Henry IV, Part I
Henry V
Hiroshima
The Hobbit
The House on Mango
   Street
I Know Why the Caged
   Bird Sings
The Iliad
The Importance of
   Being Earnest
Inferno
Invisible Man
Jane Eyre
Johnny Tremain
The Joy Luck Club
Julius Caesar

The Jungle
The Killer Angels
King Lear
The Last of the
   Mohicans
Les Misérables
A Lesson Before Dying
Little Women
Lord of the Flies
Macbeth
Madame Bovary
The Merchant of
   Venice
A Midsummer Night's
   Dream
Moby-Dick
Much Ado About
   Nothing
My Ántonia
Narrative of the Life of
   Frederick Douglass
Native Son
The New Testament
Night
The Odyssey
Oedipus Plays
Of Mice and Men
The Old Man and
   the Sea
The Old Testament
Oliver Twist
The Once and Future
   King
One Flew Over the
   Cuckoo's Nest
One Hundred Years of
   Solitude
Othello
Our Town
The Outsiders
Paradise Lost
The Pearl
The Picture of Dorian
   Gray
Poe's Short Stories
A Portrait of the Artist
   as a Young Man

Pride and Prejudice
The Prince
A Raisin in the Sun
The Red Badge of
   Courage
The Republic
The Return of the King
Richard III
Robinson Crusoe
Romeo and Juliet
Scarlet Letter
A Separate Peace
Silas Marner
Sir Gawain and the
   Green Knight
Slaughterhouse-Five
Song of Solomon
The Sound and the
   Fury
The Stranger
A Streetcar Named
   Desire
The Sun Also Rises
A Tale of Two Cities
The Taming of the
   Shrew
The Tempest
Tess of the
   d'Urbervilles
The Things They
   Carried
The Two Towers
Their Eyes Were
   Watching God
Things Fall Apart
To Kill a Mockingbird
Treasure Island
Twelfth Night
Ulysses
Uncle Tom's Cabin
Walden
War and Peace
Wuthering Heights
A Yellow Raft in Blue
   Water

Visit sparknotes.com for many more!